SEA SALT

SEA SALT

FABRIZIO AIELLI

With CHELLE KOSTER WALTON
Photography by VANESSA ROGERS
Design by FRANK RUSSELL

SEA SALT

www.seasaltnaples.com

Published in the United States by Story Farm, LLC.
www.story-farm.com

Library of Congress Cataloging-in-Publication Data is available upon request.
ISBN 978-0-9905205-0-4

Printed in China

Editorial director: Ashley Fraxedas
Art director: Frank Russell
Photography: Vanessa Rogers
Project manager: Tanya Buchanan
Head motivator: Ingrid Aielli
Copy editors: Eva Dougherty, Rona Gindin, Veronica Randall
Recipe testers: Chelle Koster Walton, Victoria Allman, Bernice Rodriguez
Recipe staging: Jason Goddard
Indexing: Heidi Blough
Production management: Tina Dahl

10 9 8 7 6 5 4 3 2 1
First Edition

story farm

"MY WIFE, INGRID, IS THE FIRE UNDER THE POT ON MY STOVE. IT'S WHAT DRIVES ME EVERY DAY."

This book is also dedicated to the memory of Nane Jan Kimijan, who thought he didn't know how to cook but was mistaken.

CONTENTS

01 FOREWORD

02 WELCOME

13 SALT OF THE EARTH

14 STARTERS

38 SALADS

64 SOUPS

80 PASTA

114 FISH

142 MEAT AND POULTRY

164 BAR SANDWICHES

180 PASTRIES AND DESSERTS

200 COCKTAILS

208 PANTRY

214 SEA SALT TEAM

216 INDEX

FOREWORD

by Colman Andrews

The southwestern Florida community of Naples has little in common with its Italian namesake, beyond palm trees, ample sunshine and the proximity of salt water. Italy's Naples is frenetic, crime-ridden, sense-assaulting, sometimes crazy fun; Florida's is calm and safe, caressing the senses rather than assaulting them, and the fun is easygoing. That no doubt helps explain why tourism is the most important industry in Naples (the Florida one) and why it's home to the second-highest concentration of millionaires in America. It also helps explain why, after several years of visiting the city, an Italian chef/restaurateur named Fabrizio Aielli from Venice (the Italian one) and his Slovakian-born wife and co-restaurateur, named Ingrid, made the very smart decision to buy a house and open a gelateria there early in the 2000s and then to move permanently in 2007.

The Aiellis had made a name for themselves in the American restaurant world with a succession of three popular establishments in Washington, D.C., all named after the celebrated 18th-century Venetian playwright and librettist Carlo Goldoni—Goldoni, Osteria Goldoni and Teatro Goldoni. They liked Washington and were well-liked in return, but when they started spending time in Naples (my food-loving, formerly D.C.-based in-laws, who have a house in Naples, got them there the first time after Ingrid complained that she could never get Fabrizio to take a vacation) they were seduced by its many charms. I also have a highly speculative theory that at some point, probably on some dark, snowy afternoon in January, Fabrizio and Ingrid looked at each other and said "Slovakia? The Veneto? Washington? Why can't we move someplace where the sky is blue and we don't need overcoats?"

Of course, it was a given that the Aiellis would open a restaurant in their new home. Historic Third Street South, the heart of what locals fondly call Old Naples (it dates back more than a century, old by Florida standards), already had some good restaurants, but the couple found a great location in the middle of the Third Street shopping district and, in 2008, opened not another Italian restaurant but, well, an Aiellian place, called Sea Salt. It has been wildly popular with both locals and the tourist trade from the day it opened and has energized—and raised the bar for—not just the local dining scene but the Florida dining landscape in general.

There are Italian notes on Sea Salt's menu—good Parma ham, some pasta dishes (though not many more than you'd find on a lot of American menus these days)—but the main focus is on absolutely first-rate fish and shellfish from Florida and beyond (including what is almost certainly the region's best and biggest selection of oysters), cooked simply but with just enough elaboration to let you know that there's a master in the kitchen (and Fabrizio is always in the kitchen). Perfect produce, treated with flair, fills out the plates, and, oh, most dishes are seasoned with judicious applications of sea salt, from a larder stocked with 100 or more varieties.

In 2012, Fabrizio and Ingrid opened their second restaurant, just down the street, this one unabashedly Italian—a lively trattoria called Barbatella dispensing heroic quantities of pasta, along with carpaccio, mixed fried seafood, Italian-style lamb chops and other peninsular delights, including pizza so good that it should make the other Naples just a little nervous.

Everybody loves Italian food, Fabrizio and Ingrid probably even more than the rest of us, but It is at Sea Salt that Fabrizio has the opportunity to really shine and to put to use his decades of cooking experience and all he has learned through his ceaseless curiosity about other cuisines and culinary techniques, without worrying about regional accents. At Sea Salt—and with this book—Fabrizio reminds us that he is a chef, not just an Italian one.

— Colman Andrews is the editorial director of TheDailyMeal.com and author of The Country Cooking of Italy, The Taste of America, My Usual Table: A Life in Restaurants *and five other books on food.*

WELCOME

My Recipes, Your Recipes

WELCOME TO MY COOKBOOK, which I share with you as I share my dishes at Sea Salt and Barbatella in Old Naples, Florida. I hope you love "armchair cooking" along with me, maybe even trying some of the recipes. But please: don't believe you are going to learn how to cook from my cookbook. What you will learn about is my passion for food.

Every recipe tells a story and takes you with me on a small mind-journey of food memories, visions of new flavors and the elemental simplicity of cooking from the heart.

I cook by touch and smell and taste. In your own kitchen, you should not be intimidated; you should relax and develop your own rhythm and senses by getting in touch with the different elements of cuisine.

The recipes herein that I so happily share with you are not static or set in stone. I change them every time I make them, and so should you. They are our recipes, not mine alone.

I love to record recipes in my mind and then every time try to always do them better. Sometimes when you write down a recipe and just follow it, you're stuck with it. Cooking should be a creative process, not an exercise in following directions. I want to put my recipes in your mind and let you customize them. Do not become too structured: let your mind go.

My recipe ideas come from many places: my dreams, a night at the opera, a childhood treat I remember from Venice, a Pink Floyd song, sharing a meal with a friend, traveling the world. A question in my mind: what if I tried it this way? For example, you will see my sea urchin carbonara recipe in the Pasta section. Sea urchin is sweet and cured pork is salty, so the two complement each other. So I think, why not try it? Then every time I make it depending on my mood, my own cravings, even the weather, I make little changes. I tweak it.

First you create, and after you evolve. Without creation, there is no evolution

If you cannot find one of the ingredients listed in a recipe, or it's out of season, or you simply don't like it, just use your imagination a little and think about how you can tweak it. Make it your own.

Diners in my restaurants come and tell me they're so nervous about cooking for guests. I tell

them to have a glass of wine and relax, and then the cooking will come naturally. "If it's stressful, you shouldn't cook," I say. Then they come back and tell me, "But Fabrizio, I had three glasses of wine, and now I can't cook." I tell them to relax and call someone to order food.

When friends ask me what they should cook, I tell them, "Prepare what you know best. Make something that is part of your history, your growing up, your experience. Then it will be meaningful. You and your guests will be at ease."

It should never be stressful. Cooking should be joy you share with your family and friends. You can serve something simple like sandwiches made from chicken you roasted the day before. Dress them with my tomato marmalade or pickled red onions to make them special. Use a good bread. It doesn't have to be complicated to be delicious. If you don't have time to make your own special condiments, you can find wonderful products these days in gourmet shops and online.

If you are in a bad mood or stressed out when you are cooking, it shows in the result. You bruise the fruits and vegetables you touch. Everything feels forced, and it will be difficult to please even yourself.

I always say: "Cook with a glass of wine and a smile on your face." Everything tastes much better.

JOURNEY OF A CHEF

I have traveled around the world during my career as a chef. When you travel by car from country to country in Europe, there's always that time commitment and bother of going through customs. I equate cooking to traveling by airplane. To flying. There are no borders, no customs to slow you down mid-journey. You can be free in your thinking. There are no rules. Every whim is worth a try. You can start your meal in Asia, then travel to Italy or France for your main course, and finish in the Caribbean islands. No passport, no border patrols.

I can have 100 recipes flitting through my brain in a minute's time. Luckily I forget most of them within the next four minutes. The rest I try, and change, and change again. Every time I read a recipe in this book, I have a dozen ideas on how to make it different. My publisher joked with me when I told him this. He said, "Fabrizio, you can't keep changing the recipes! We've already photographed the dishes."

I tell you this because I want you to know that cooking travels. It, too, travels around the world. It flies as quickly as an idea. Follow it where it takes you.

I began from modest beginnings in Venice, Italy. We lived simply, we ate simply. We fished for a lot of our food. We grew our own vegetables. I started cooking at a young age. The biggest influences on my cooking? My mother, my mother's sister, my grandmother, my neighbor.

My cooking career began in Venice, later moving away to gain experience in some of the finest restaurants and hotels around the world. In 1989 I was working on the Caribbean island of St. Maarten when I had to return home to take care of some paperwork. The day I went to the Italian courthouse, it was closed because one of the floors had collapsed so I had to stay in Europe longer. That was a stroke of good fate, because I ran into a friend who invited me to his wedding in former Czechoslovakia, and that's where I met my wife-to-be, Ingrid. We fell in love, and I never returned to the Caribbean. We couldn't leave because at that time the Berlin Wall was coming down, and it was too difficult for Ingrid, a Slovak citizen, to leave Europe.

When things quieted down in Europe, we moved to Washington, D.C., and were married on February 15, 1990. It was a small wedding and we celebrated with pizza. After a few months, Ingrid got homesick, so we returned to Venice, where we had a big church wedding. I worked as executive chef in several different Venetian restaurants. After a couple of years, we were ready to move back to the States.

Here in the U.S., I found what I consider my favorite style of cuisine. I love what used to be called "Innovative American Cuisine," because it is all about the best of every cuisine: Italian, French, Asian. There are no borders! Everything is open to you. No one thinks you are crazy to combine different things. It's very open-minded. It leaves room for surprise. That's one of my favorite things: surprising my guests into a new way of looking at food. It started in California, but now it's really just known as "new American" or "global cuisine." It represents the beauty of America. It is a reflection of the melting pot of cultures that created this nation.

Upon embracing the freshness and freedom of the California culinary school of thought, I moved to Washington, D.C., in 1992 and felt excited, inspired to exercise my own imagination and sometimes "crazy" ideas. In 1995, Ingrid and I opened the first of our own restaurants, Goldoni, followed by Osteria Goldoni in 1998 and Teatro Goldoni in 1999. We named the restaurants for Carlo Goldoni, a witty 18th-century playwright whose plays often involved food. Goldoni was quite a character himself in his time, a man who loved to cook, eat and entertain.

Ingrid and I first visited Naples, on the west coast of Florida, in 2001. Here, we discovered a city on the water that made me feel immediately at home, as it was so much like Venice. We fell in love with the town, the beach, the sea. We immediately wanted to live here, and so in 2007 we moved permanently to Naples to embark upon our next adventure in fine dining. We walked into a landmark building on Third Street South and knew immediately that it was the right place for our restaurant.

Sea Salt opened in November of 2008, inspired by the Gulf of Mexico. I wanted to wield the element of surprise. So I created a menu that could evolve with the seasons, with what was, with the 100 ideas in my head.

Then in 2012, we had the opportunity to open Barbatella just down the street. I envisioned this as a spirited Italian trattoria. More casual, more communal. Here I can stay close to the Italian traditions of my childhood, the elements that struck a chord with the cuisine I most associated with Italy: the pizza, the pasta, the meatballs, the cheese and sausages, the gelato.

In the fall of 2014, we anticipate opening a second Sea Salt in downtown St. Petersburg, Florida. It will be basically the same concept with a new twist: a special oven to bake oysters. You can select the variety of oyster you want and we can prepare it 70 different ways. So the oyster becomes almost like a pizza dough shell upon which we can create, well, almost anything you can imagine!

At all of my restaurants, we are forever changing. Not because I feel a need to make dishes better, but because of my excitement and passion for food. Every time I envision change, I get as excited

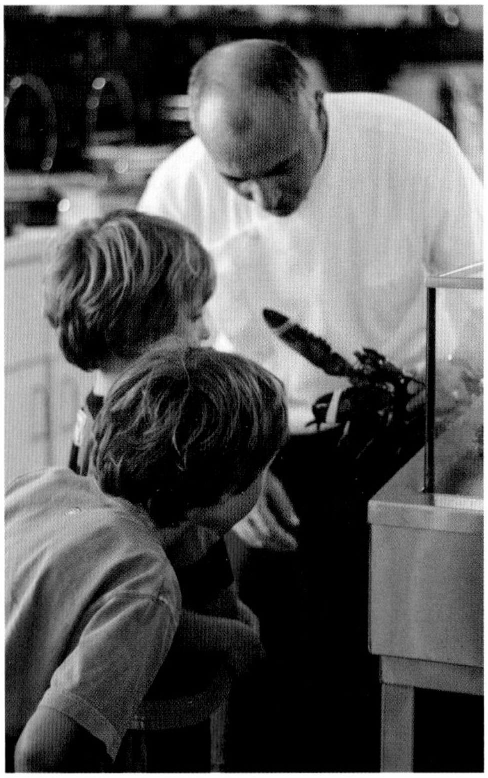

as when I first created a dish. I make it 10 or so times, and then it becomes yesterday.

My style of cooking, however, has always stayed the same. Times change, trends change, seasons change, technology changes, people's culinary sophistication changes. And so do my dishes accordingly.

When I first opened Sea Salt, the media wanted to know how I termed my cooking. They picked up on "Venetian world cuisine," because I wanted to equate my style with that freedom of travel. I wanted it to be like Marco Polo, picking up influences along the way. But I don't often really use the term Venetian world cuisine myself; I describe my style as just cooking. Pure. Simple. Elemental.

A DAY IN THE LIFE OF A CHEF

So that you understand what it's like to be a chef who starts, owns and runs his own restaurants, let me tell you a little bit about my typical day. There's really no such thing as a typical day because every day is different. You must wear a lot of hats, other than a toque, when you are a chef and restaurant owner. You become a businessman, which is almost completely opposite a chef's mentality. You must also be a good host, and that's one of my favorite parts of the job. I love talking to my customers. People who love good food are often well-traveled and so interesting. We have in common our love of food, wine and seeing and tasting the world.

But back to my day. Every chef goes about his or her day in a slightly different way, but basically we are the same. I start by taking 20 minutes for myself to get my thoughts in order. I have a simple, energizing breakfast of a blended "cocktail" of organic acai juice, freeze-dried goji berries from the Himalayas, organic chia, liquid garlic and turmeric. No coffee, no milk.

Ingrid tells me, "It's another beautiful day." She is the fire under the pot on the stove. It's what drives me every day. I get in my car, and listen either to opera or Pink Floyd. Then I'm ready for my day.

When I arrive at the restaurant around 11 a.m., I walk from back to front to say good morning to everybody: from the hostess and bartender up front to my kitchen crew and service staff. I go back to my office to change into my chef attire and then consult with my executive chef, Jason Goddard. Sometimes we argue lightheartedly because he's a talented chef. He really understands me. Like, we will talk about the day's special, and I will tease: "Why no rabbit?" He says, "We have no rabbit." So the next day he'll order rabbit, and I'll ask him, "Why rabbit today?" So we have fun, and we disagree sometimes. That's okay. It's not good to agree on everything.

We always talk about today—yesterday is forgotten. We discuss what he will order for tomorrow because we change things on the menu daily to showcase what we are able to get fresh. I mostly love being in the kitchen, but running restaurants requires office time. I must take a couple of hours each day to take care of business, review how we are doing, call companies I deal with.

As soon as lunch service is over, we start preparing for dinner. That's our big "showtime." During lunch and dinner, I like to walk around the restaurant and speak with the guests, greet those who return again and again and have become friends. I get such great energy talking to them, meeting their families. Sometimes I must talk to customers who are unhappy about something. I think usually they are unhappy before they sit down in my restaurant, and I say to myself: No one should go out for a fine dinner without a positive attitude about the day and the experience they will have. I describe the time and talent that goes into each dish so they can understand how much effort goes into making their dining experience a pleasurable one. I am so happy to see our customers leave with smiles.

It makes it all worthwhile—the hard work and the balancing between ideas and numbers that are required for opening a restaurant of your own. It's different from working for another restaurant owner because you are the one inventing the concept, and then communicating it in your menu, to your architect and interior designer, and to your chef and staff. Starting a new restaurant is exciting, but also challenging, as you try to make all the pieces of the puzzle fit. Sometimes, you push to make one piece fit where it doesn't belong, until you realize it just won't work. But when it does all come together, it's a beautiful thing!

I love my work. I am very proud of what I do, and I wouldn't change a thing. I always tell people I am so happy at work and smiling so much that the first muscles I must relax when I go home are the muscles in my face. Of course I get upset and angry, too, as my staff reminds me—because that happens when you are passionate about quality and perfection.

ADJUSTING AT-HOME TECHNIQUES

It is easy for us at Sea Salt to make the recipes you will find on the pages that follow because we have the equipment and the staff to help us. We use basic book recipes; they are in our heads and always changing and evolving depending on what comes in fresh that morning and what we dreamed up in the night. We are kind of like car or smartphone engineers that way, always looking how to improve and update our products so they are better and more innovative than the rest.

I remember that my mom never used recipes, either. She knew everything by heart, and heart is what it takes to make a good cook. So don't worry about these recipes too much. They are only ideas that you should consult. If you don't have a certain ingredient, substitute with another. Don't worry about weighing and

"FIRST YOU CREATE, AND AFTER YOU EVOLVE.
WITHOUT CREATION, THERE IS NO EVOLUTION."

"THE RECIPES ARE IN OUR HEADS AND ALWAYS CHANGING AND EVOLVING WITH WHAT COMES IN FRESH THAT DAY AND WHAT WE DREAMED UP IN THE NIGHT."

"THE BEST WAY TO WEIGH AND MEASURE IS WITH YOUR EYES AND HANDS. **CREATING A DISH IS LIKE CREATING A WORK OF ART. ONCE IT IS CREATED, EVERYTHING AFTER IS A REPRODUCTION OF THE ORIGINAL CREATION."**

measuring every ingredient, except in baking. The best way to weigh and measure is with your eyes and hands. Creating a dish is like creating a work of art. Once it is created, everything after is a reproduction of the original creation.

We make everything from scratch here because we want to and we can. It's what we do; it's our business. When I'm at home on my day off, I don't need to cook everything from A to Z. It's easy, I just call the restaurant and ask my chefs for a sauce. But you should take shortcuts when you don't have the time or you don't feel like spending it in the kitchen. Buy your pasta, stocks and other components ready-made to help you out. You can find some wonderful prepared sauces and other ingredients these days. Don't make yourself crazy thinking you have to cook it all like Fabrizio cooks it.

For instance, in the restaurant, we sometimes flash-fry tarragon or lavender as a garnish because we have the deep-fryer operating, so it is easy to do, and it's a nice touch. At home, it would mean another step, another pot and more time. You can just use the fresh herbs as a garnish, or don't worry about it if you have no tarragon or lavender on hand.

Some dishes require a slow hand in the prep kitchen, where we simmer our stocks for hours and carefully craft our basic sauces. They are the building blocks for the à la minute dishes we make to order for our guests. We design these dishes so that we can prepare meals in a timely manner. As experts in this department, we flash-cook fish and meats at high temperatures with grapeseed oil, which has a high smoking point and lends wonderful flavor to whatever is sautéed in it. The high temperature also seals in flavor and instantly caramelizes. If you wish, you can use a lower temperature to reduce splattering.

Another method that helps us with our style of cooking is the sous vide, a sort of an upside-down cooking process. You pack the meat or fish with herbs and seasonings in a sealable bag, then cook it very slowly in a machine that is sort of like a Jacuzzi for food. Then you sear it at a high heat before serving for a tender inside, crusted outside.

The sealing element of the sous-vide equipment is quite costly for a home cook to purchase, but that does not mean you cannot adapt my recipes to your kitchen.

Of course, a pasta machine is essential to us at Sea Salt, and home pasta machines are inexpensive for cooks who really love pasta made fresh. But there are also ways of making pasta without a machine, and many Italian markets will make it for you. Some will even customize it for you if you want, say by adding saffron or chocolate, to duplicate recipes that I am giving you. Or change the recipes to flavors you prefer. Because remember, once you have made one and given it your own style, that recipe is now yours, not mine.

Foremost, and I cannot emphasize this enough: Enjoy yourself in the kitchen. If you are not enjoying yourself, stop cooking. If you are enjoying yourself, your guests are going to love whatever you serve them, because it is a piece of yourself and your imagination they are tasting.

A WORD ABOUT INGREDIENTS

One thing I advise that you do not skimp on in your kitchen is the quality of the ingredients. Quality products are not only more flavorful, but also more nutritious and healthy. But that doesn't mean they have to be expensive.

Quality ingredients are the foundation for a wonderful meal. The better your ingredients, the simpler your meal can be. A beautiful, ripe tomato, for instance, can be its own meal with a little high-quality olive oil and salt, or some bread or cheese.

When you are shopping for a special dinner with guests and you think you're going to buy all your ingredients in one store, good luck. Your guests will appreciate the extra effort, and you're going to see the smiles on their faces.

SALT OF THE EARTH

. . . and the Sea

At Sea Salt, we start diners out with a trio of imported salts and extra-virgin olive oil served with the bread course. So immediately, they have an introduction to our central sea-salt concept. The sampling varies from among our 130 different types and flavors of salt. The tray may contain, for instance, a combo of *kala namak* from India, *sel gris* from France and *alaea* red clay salt from Hawaii. Upon request, we also give the option of a six-flavor flight of salt, and that's very popular for those who want to sample and experiment with how the salts interact with different dishes.

Besides sea salts and land foundation salts from around the world, we feature artisanal salts into which we infuse flavors using Himalayan pink or Sicilian Trapani salts. We infuse them with chipotle, espresso, Spanish rosemary, wild porcini, green tea, lemon twist, vintage Merlot, white truffle, garlic—we've got all kinds of different salts.

When we first opened, there was no other place I knew of that was featuring salt to this extent. In my Washington, D.C., restaurants, we were already using 10 different types of salt. Today, we go through more than 2,400 pounds of salt each year between the kitchen and our retail shop. The concept for Sea Salt came to me one night while I was in the planning stages of my first Naples restaurant. I woke up in the morning and said to my wife, "I want to do something with sea salt. We're close to the water; it makes sense."

I did research to learn more about salt. One thing I discovered was salt's healthful, healing properties. I know there's a huge debate about whether salt is good for you, but I found out our bodies actually need salt. Not the bad salt that's processed or added to preserved and canned foods, but good, natural salt.

People go to the spa and spend a lot for a salt bath because it is good for certain skin conditions such as eczema and psoriasis. If you cut yourself and put salt on it, it will sting, but it will cure it. Salt kills bacteria and is known to strengthen the immune system. Sea salt contains potassium, which can prevent muscle spasms. Incredibly, sea salt has achieved positive results in treating asthma, high cholesterol, hypertension, depression, osteoporosis and obesity.

In food, just a little pinch of sea salt or flavor-infused salt can elevate a dish. It brings out the best of food's natural flavors. But like everything else, it is best enjoyed in moderation, in small pinches. You will see in my recipes that I always list sea salt for the sodium component in the ingredient list. You may want to get creative and try different salts and infused salts with different recipes.

Our natural salts come from around the world—El Salvador's Mayan sun, Mediterranean *sel de mer*, Sonoma sea salt, Australia's Murray River pink salt flakes, Himalayan pink salt, Bali's pyramid salt, Mexico's *flor blanca*, Bolivia's *rose* salt and others.

All the natural salts have their own textures and characteristics. The coarser salts add crunch, while others have a fine, silky texture.

We also serve infused salts to complement our cocktails. Here are some of my suggestions for pairing infused salts with dishes you prepare at home:

Matcha (green tea) salt: Try it on scrambled eggs, steamed fish, chocolate and desserts.

Lemon twist salt: This is an essential salt for seafood lovers, bartenders and pastry chefs.

Vermont maple sea salt: Top off your popcorn or ice cream; add a new dimension to grilled pork.

Black truffle salt: It adds a hint of earthy, mushroom flavor to beef, eggs, potatoes and pasta.

Ghost pepper salt: For flaming flavor, sprinkle over chicken wings, chili or fajitas.

Espresso brava salt: It's a delicious match with a cognac reduction or anything with nutmeg, anise, vanilla, cherry, hazelnut or raspberry flavors.

Lime fresco salt: Use to rim a drinking glass, sprinkle on chicken or fish before grilling, or add to a salad.

Sun-ripened tomato salt: It's great for soups and sauces or mixed with herbs for a spice rub.

Thai ginger salt: Combine the clean, simple flavor of sea salt with fresh, juicy ginger. The ginger flavor of this fusion variety cannot be matched by powdered or synthetic flavorings. Use on grilled veggies, Asian noodles or fish.

Some infused salts, such as jalapeño pepper and toasted onion, really go well with anything. Try using them as glass rimmers when making Bloody Marys. Experiment by mixing and matching for different effects.

Salt is just one more dimension you can add to your cooking's flavor profile. Enjoy the sea salt and its benefits. Like the sea, it's a part of our makeup and, here in Florida, our life.

As John F. Kennedy once said: "... All of us have in our veins the exact same percentage of salt in our blood that exists in the ocean, and, therefore, we have salt in our blood, in our sweat, in our tears. We are tied to the ocean."

STARTERS

FIRST IMPRESSIONS

A Warm Welcome

‡

To make sure our guests at Sea Salt and Barbatella have the best possible dining experience, we must properly prepare them for the meal that lies ahead. We greet them warmly at the door and make them feel welcome. We help them feel at ease with conversation and a glass of wine. We tingle their sense of smell with wonderful aromas from the kitchen and prepare their imaginations by offering a menu that excites their minds. Then we reward their palates.

The appetizer offers our guests a first impression of the dining experience they are about to have. Since diners remember best the first and last courses they eat, the success of the appetizer is crucial. If I serve you an appetizer that isn't well thought out and carefully presented, the meal is over.

When you are making a meal in your home for guests, you must remember balance. I once prepared a meal at my chef's table for a man who told me he loved lobster above all else. I knew I would serve him lobster in the main course, but I also wanted to whet his taste for lobster in the appetizer. I presented him a plate composed of persimmons, candied chestnuts, crispy chives and plainly steamed nuggets of lobster. He was amazed at the way the progression of simple ingredients, when eaten first, complemented the lobster. Although the dish had lobster, it wasn't all about the lobster; it was about balance and the interplay of flavors. I was educating his taste, evolving his palate in preparation for the dish to come.

Prepare your guests with an appetizer that's a little playful and balanced. I like to drizzle sauces on the plate that spark the taste buds and give the guests a little mystery. "Mmm, what is that taste?" they wonder. Now they're not simply chewing food. They are trying to understand flavors and how they interact with each other. Their palates are ready to open, to expand with the simplicity of flavors but complexity of combined tastes. Bring on the next course!

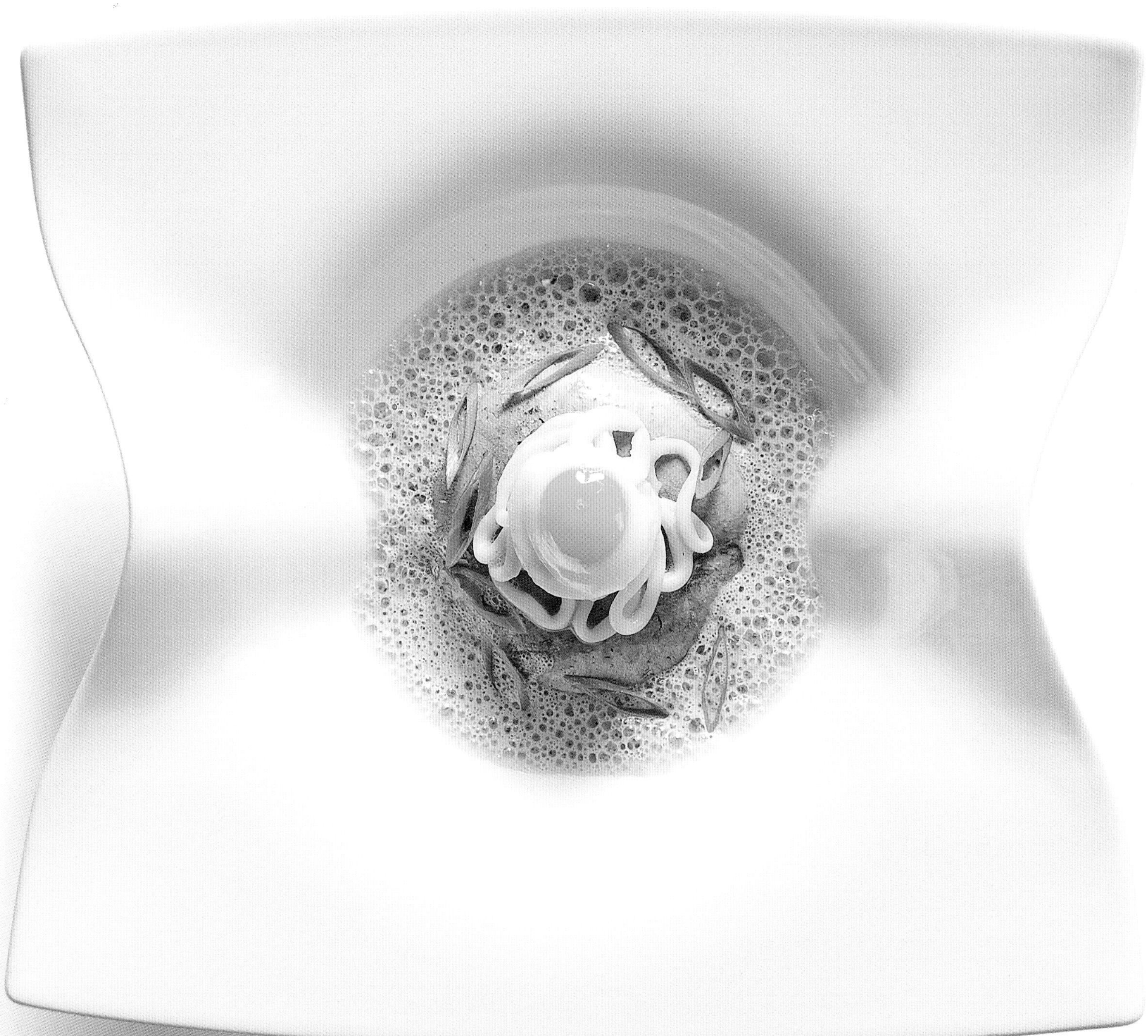

CALAMARI WITH PORTOBELLO CAPPUCCINO AND QUAIL EGG

We have fun with this dish, grinding Portobello mushrooms and preparing them like coffee, then using butter instead of milk to create the cappuccino-style froth. As for the quail eggs, I intended to use them in another dish and inadvertently put them in this one. It worked—a happy kitchen accident!

Serves 6

PORTOBELLO CAPPUCCINO

10 ounces Portobello mushrooms, broken into chunks (about 2 cups)
1 tablespoon garlic, chopped
1 quart water
⅓ cup tamari or soy sauce
½ cup cold butter, cubed
Sea salt, to taste
Freshly ground white peppercorns, to taste

CALAMARI

6 quail eggs
2 teaspoons garlic, minced
⅓ cup extra-virgin olive oil
1 tablespoon chives, chopped, divided, half for garnish
1 tablespoon spring onion, finely cut
1½ pounds fresh calamari tubes, sliced into ⅛-inch rings
½ teaspoon sea salt
¼ teaspoon freshly ground pepper

PREPARE PORTOBELLO CAPPUCCINO

In a food processor, puree portobellos, garlic, water and soy sauce. Pour into a small saucepan and cook on medium heat to reduce by two-thirds. Pass through a fine mesh filter and discard pulp. Just before plating, blend liquid, salt, pepper and add butter a little at a time in a blender on high. Blend for 1½ to 2 minutes until foam is produced.

PREPARE CALAMARI

In nonstick sauté pan on medium heat, cook the eggs sunny-side up and reserve for plating. Preheat a large sauté pan to medium-high heat. In a mixing bowl, mix together garlic, olive oil, chives, spring onion, calamari, salt and pepper. Transfer to a sauté pan and cook very quickly, about 1 to 1½ minutes or until calamari rings turn white.

ASSEMBLE

Divide the cappuccino among 6 shallow bowls. Add sautéed calamari into center of cappuccino and top with quail egg. Garnish with chives.

PARMA PROSCIUTTO, FIGS, PARMESAN CRISPS, PISTACHIO AND ARUGULA WITH TOMATO MARMALADE

Figs and prosciutto were made for each other. Pistachios and tomato marmalade add not only bright color to this dish but also texture and sweetness. And for all the elegance it brings, the Parmesan crisp, which is almost like a cracker, is easy to make.

Serves 6

PARMESAN CRISPS

4 ounces Parmesan, freshly grated

DRESSING

2 tablespoons extra-virgin olive oil
1 teaspoon lemon juice
Salt to taste
1 pinch pepper

SALAD

2 ounces arugula, washed and dried
1 tablespoon sun-dried tomato in olive oil, brunoise
7 ounces Parma prosciutto, very thinly sliced
9 Black Mission figs, quartered

GARNISH

½ cup Sicilian Pistachio Paste (page 211)
2 tablespoons Tomato Marmalade (page 212)

PREPARE PARMESAN CRISPS

Heat stovetop burner to medium high and place 18-inch nonstick pan on it for 2 minutes. Remove pan from heat. Spoon one-sixth of grated Parmesan into pan, shaking the pan to distribute cheese evenly over the bottom. Return to burner for about 1½ minutes or until the cheese bubbles and the edges turn brown. Gently lift with a spatula at the edges and flip the cheese to continue browning for another minute or so, until the cheese begins to harden. Slide the cheese from the pan and cut in 4 strips. Repeat process five more times to make 4 slices for each salad.

PREPARE SALAD

Whisk together olive oil and lemon juice until blended. Add salt and pepper. Toss together arugula, tomatoes and dressing.

ASSEMBLE

Divide prosciutto among 6 plates. Top with arugula-tomato salad. Arrange fig quarters around salad and add dabs of pistachio paste and tomato marmalade on top.

KUMAMOTO OYSTERS ON A FOGGY DAY IN VENICE

I got my inspiration for this one day while walking around Venice. A winter fog started to creep in over a couple sitting outside a restaurant eating fresh oysters. It was such a magical scene that I wanted to recreate that moment—on a plate. This dish conjures that cold day in Venice. In addition to the fog, I use pomegranates and persimmons, which are sure signs of winter when you see them appear in a grocer's window.

Serves 6

YUZU FOAM

½ cup yuzu juice
½ cup pomegranate juice
1 tablespoon sugar
Salt, to taste
2 tablespoons Versawhip
1 teaspoon xanthan gum

OYSTERS

18 Kumamoto oysters
1 tablespoon fresh persimmons
1 teaspoon chives
½ teaspoon olive oil
½ tablespoon pink peppercorns

FOG

½ pound dry ice
Crushed ice
1 cup blue Curaçao liqueur
1 cup water

PREPARE YUZU FOAM

Combine all ingredients and blend with an immersion blender until completely aerated. Place inside the canister of an iSi siphon and charge, following manufacturer's directions.

PREPARE OYSTERS

Shuck oysters, leaving them on the half shell and detaching foot from shell. Dice persimmons and chives and toss with oil. Top each oyster with persimmon-chive mixture and pink peppercorns. Finish with a dollop of yuzu foam from the siphon.

ASSEMBLE

Divide dry ice among 6 bowls and top with crushed ice. Place oysters on top of crushed ice. Combine Curaçao and water and place in a teapot. Pour Curaçao over the ice tableside to activate dry ice and create the fog.

**Note: Dry ice is extremely cold and can cause frostbite. Always use leather gloves or a kitchen towel when handling dry ice.*

SEA URCHIN, LOBSTER AND SCALLOPS WITH BRAISED POTATO AND LARDO

I consider sea urchins to be the foie gras of the sea. They possess an elegant sweetness, as does the lardo. Together, they create one of most exquisite combinations imaginable.

Serves 6

SALAD

3 (1¼-pound) lobsters
6 U10 dry pack sea scallops
1 ounce parsley, chopped
½ cup cherry tomatoes, halved
¼ cup olive oil
1 teaspoon lemon juice
Salt, to taste
White pepper, to taste

BRAISED POTATO

10 ounces red Russet potatoes, sliced ⅛-inch thick
4 cups Chicken Stock (page 209)
1 tablespoon Pernod
1 tablespoon salt
½ cup white balsamic vinegar
2 bay leaves
2 peels lemon zest
2 cups ice cubes

SEA URCHIN SAUCE

¾ cup Lobster Stock (page 210)
2 ounces sea urchins
2 tablespoons lemon juice
½ cup grapeseed oil
1 teaspoon salt
1½ teaspoons soy lecithin

FOR ASSEMBLY

6 sea urchins
4 ounces lardo Colonnata, thinly sliced, or fat of bacon, or salted pork
6 stems dill, chopped
18 medium basil leaves

PREPARE SALAD

Steam lobster over simmering water for 5 to 6 minutes. Cool and remove meat from shell. Slice the meat thinly. Reserve at room temperature. Steam scallops in the same pot for 2 to 3 minutes. Toss lobster and scallops with parsley, tomatoes, oil, lemon juice, salt and pepper. Keep warm.

PREPARE BRAISED POTATOES

Place potatoes, chicken stock, Pernod, salt, vinegar, bay leaves and lemon zest in a pot. Bring to a boil and cook over high heat for 7 to 10 minutes. Lower heat and simmer until potatoes are soft. Remove from heat and add ice to cool. Remove potatoes from liquid and set aside. Keep warm.

PREPARE SAUCE

In a blender, blend stock, sea urchins, lemon juice, grapeseed oil and salt on high speed for 30 seconds. Add soy lecithin and blend on high until foamy.

ASSEMBLE

Warm 6 plates. Place half a lobster tail, 1 scallop, 1 sea urchin and 3 to 4 slices potato onto each plate. Drizzle sauce over seafood. Lay 1 slice lardo on top of warm seafood. Garnish with dill, olive oil and basil leaves.

BEEF CARPACCIO AND UBRIACO CHEESE WITH TROPICAL TRUFFLE AND TEQUILA—JALAPEÑO SAUCE

One day in the kitchen I was experimenting with raw heart of palm, which comes from the sabal palm, Florida's state tree. It reminded me of white truffle as I shaved it, and so I called it "tropical truffle." While swamp cabbage, as it's also called, is an old Florida pioneer food, it's very elegant in its raw form and adds a touch of mystery to this dish.

Serves 6

SAUCE

1 cup Mayonnaise (page 210)
3 tablespoons tequila
1 tablespoon lime juice
1 tablespoon lemon juice
1 tablespoon jalapeño, minced
½ teaspoon Worcestershire sauce
Sea salt, to taste

CARPACCIO

12 ounces beef tenderloin

FOR ASSEMBLY

3 (4-inch) pieces hearts of palm
4 ounces Ubriaco cheese
2 ounces baby kale
1 tablespoon green onion, chopped
3 tablespoons extra-virgin olive oil
1 jalapeño, sliced and seeded
Sea salt, to taste

PREPARE SAUCE

Mix together mayonnaise, tequila, juices, jalapeño, Worcestershire and salt. Let sit to meld flavors.

PREPARE CARPACCIO

Place tenderloin in freezer until it begins to harden. Slice very thin and reserve for plating. (Alternatively, you can ask your butcher to slice carpaccio-style.)

ASSEMBLE

Divide tenderloin slices among 6 plates. Using a truffle mandoline, thinly slice hearts of palm and arrange on top of beef. Shave cheese on top of beef. Garnish with baby kale and chopped onion. Drizzle tequila sauce over beef and finish with olive oil, jalapeño and salt.

FOIE GRAS PEANUT BUTTER TERRINE WITH BALSAMIC MUST AND RASPBERRY JELLY

While this might seem like a complicated dish, it's really not. Yes, it takes some time to bring it all together, but it's worth it. This is what I call meditation food. Just close your eyes and let your taste buds lead the way.

Serves 8

FOIE GRAS PEANUT BUTTER TERRINE

2 pounds foie gras, Grade A, sliced into 4-inch slabs
2 teaspoons Moscato Pantelleria wine
1 teaspoon cognac
½ teaspoon pink curing salt
1 tablespoon salt
1 teaspoon sugar
½ teaspoon white pepper
3 ounces creamy peanut butter
2 sheets acetate paper (8 x 8 x ¾ depth, or something similar)

RASPBERRY JELLY

2 cups Raspberry Juice (page 208)
1 teaspoon sugar
5 gelatin sheets

BALSAMIC MUST

1 tablespoon sugar
½ cup saba

GARNISH

6 ounces mâche
½ pint raspberries
Extra-virgin olive oil
Sea salt flakes

PREPARE FOIE GRAS PEANUT BUTTER TERRINE

Bring foie gras to room temperature. Mix wine, cognac, curing salt, salt, sugar, white pepper and peanut butter together in a large bowl. Coat foie gras in peanut butter mixture and place in a vacuum bag. Vacuum and seal. Let foie gras marinate in refrigerator for 24 hours. Cook sous vide at 140°F for 10 minutes, maintaining a constant temperature. Immediately place bag in an ice bath for 2 to 3 minutes, making sure the fat doesn't solidify. Remove foie gras from bag. Pass the foie gras and peanut butter through a fine-mesh sieve along with all the liquid in the bag. Whip foie gras with a spatula until creamy. Place 1 sheet acetate paper in an 8 x 8-inch cake pan. Spoon foie gras onto paper. Place another sheet on top of foie gras. Flatten to a uniform thickness of ½ inch, using a roller if necessary. Let rest in freezer until frozen.

PREPARE RASPBERRY JELLY

Bring raspberry juice and sugar to 145°F in a small saucepot. Meanwhile, soak gelatin sheets in 2 cups lukewarm water until soft. Remove gelatin and squeeze out excess liquid. Add gelatin sheets to saucepot and stir until gelatin is completely dissolved. Cool slightly. Remove terrine from freezer. Remove top sheet of acetate paper and pour raspberry liquid over foie gras. Freeze again until jelly sets, about 5 minutes. Transfer to refrigerator.

PREPARE BALSAMIC MUST

Reduce sugar and saba in a small saucepot over medium-high heat until it is the consistency of syrup. Cool.

ASSEMBLE

Place terrine on a cutting board, acetate paper down. Slice into pieces 1½ inches wide and 4 inches long. Using a spatula, transfer a slice of terrine to the center of a plate. Arrange mâche next to raspberries. Drizzle with balsamic must, oil and sea salt flakes.

CUTTLEFISH WITH BLACK-BURN ONION SAUCE, PICKLED CELERY AND RADISH

This dish reminds me of when I was a boy in Venice and we would fish for cuttlefish, which technically are mollusks. The cuttlefish blends nicely with pickled celery and the onion sauce gives the dish a sweet, smoky flavor.

Serves 6

PICKLED CELERY
1 cup water
2 tablespoons white wine vinegar
2 tablespoons pickling spices
2 tablespoons sugar
Ice cubes
1 cup celery batons

BLACK-BURN ONION SAUCE
1 cup canola oil
3 Vidalia onions, sliced
1 teaspoon salt
¼ teaspoon black pepper
3 cups Chicken Stock (page 209)
1 teaspoon squid ink

CUTTLEFISH
2 cups water
2 tablespoons white wine vinegar
1 lemon, halved
¼ cup white wine
2 bay leaves
Pinch of salt
2 pounds cuttlefish

CUTTLEFISH SALAD DRESSING
2 tablespoons lemon juice
¼ cup extra-virgin olive oil
1 tablespoon capers, chopped
2 tablespoons Italian parsley, chopped
2 tablespoons chives, chopped
Salt, to taste
Freshly ground black pepper, to taste

RADISH
1 cup ice water
1 lemon
4 red radishes

FOR ASSEMBLY
Extra-virgin olive oil

PREPARE PICKLED CELERY

Bring water, vinegar, pickling spices and sugar to a boil in a small saucepot. Lower heat to medium and simmer for 2 minutes. Add ice to cool rapidly. Add celery batons and refrigerate overnight.

PREPARE BLACK-BURN ONION SAUCE

Heat oil, onions, salt and pepper in a wide saucepan over medium-high heat. Cook, stirring occasionally, for 20 to 25 minutes, until slightly burnt. Remove ¼ cup onion and reserve. Deglaze remaining onions with stock. Add squid ink and reduce to one-third. Remove from heat and puree in a blender until smooth. Pass through a fine-mesh sieve.

PREPARE CUTTLEFISH

Bring water, vinegar, lemon halves, wine, bay leaves and salt to a simmer in a large pot. Cut cuttlefish into batons and add to pot, cooking gently for 2 to 3 minutes, depending on thickness. Cool over an ice bath, then drain and reserve fish.

PREPARE CUTTLEFISH SALAD AND DRESSING

Combine reserved cuttlefish, pickled celery, lemon juice, oil, capers, parsley, chives, salt and pepper. Toss all together and keep at room temperature.

PREPARE RADISH

Place ice water in a bowl and squeeze in lemon juice. Slice radish paper thin using a mandoline and add to ice water mixture.

ASSEMBLE

Place onion sauce on each plate and top with cuttlefish salad. Scatter radish and reserved onion around the plate and drizzle with olive oil.

OCTOPUS IN CRUSTACEAN SAUCE WITH RAISIN TOMATOES, SMOKED POTATOES AND SUMMER TRUFFLE JAM

A recent visit to Sicily reminded me how much I love octopus, and this dish unites several complementary flavors. Octopus requires long, slow simmering to make it tender. Some people say it's a myth that adding wine corks to the boiling water will help with the tenderizing process. But that's the way I've always done it—and it works!

Serves 8

RAISIN TOMATOES

1 pint cherry tomatoes
1 teaspoon salt
1 teaspoon dried oregano

SUMMER TRUFFLE JAM

2 ounces summer truffles, sliced
8 ounces black truffle juice
1 teaspoon honey
1 teaspoon lemon juice
½ teaspoon salt
1 tablespoon black truffle oil
2 tablespoons apple pectin

OCTOPUS

8 cups water
2 cups white wine
2 lemons, halved
2 tablespoons salt
½ cup white wine vinegar
4 bay leaves
2 wine corks
2–4 pounds whole octopus

CRUSTACEAN SAUCE

½ cup olive oil
2 cups onions, diced
½ tablespoon garlic, minced
2 cups celery, diced
1 cup red bell pepper, diced
6 shrimp in their shells, head on
4 lobster bodies, head and legs removed
1 tablespoon tomato paste
¼ cup Roasted Tomatoes (page 99)
3 sprigs fresh thyme
2 bay leaves
1 cup white wine
8 cups Lobster Stock (page 210)
¼ cup Pernod
1 tablespoon Worcestershire sauce
Salt, to taste
Freshly ground black pepper, to taste
4 cups heavy cream
¼ cup brandy

SMOKED POTATO

18 Yukon gold baby potatoes
¼ cup maple wood chips
1 tablespoon extra-virgin olive oil
2 tablespoons butter
Pinch of salt
Pinch of pepper

OCTOPUS SALAD

2 tablespoons extra-virgin olive oil
Pinch of salt
Pinch of white pepper

FOR ASSEMBLY

1 tablespoon black truffle oil
1 teaspoon fresh thyme leaves

PREPARE RAISIN TOMATOES

Bring a pot of water to a boil. Lightly carve an X at the base of each cherry tomato. Drop into boiling water for 15 to 20 seconds. Drain and place in ice water bath to chill. Remove from ice and peel skin using a paring knife. Toss tomatoes in a mixing bowl with salt and oregano. Place on the tray of a dehydrator and cook at 105°F for 10 hours. If you don't have a dehydrator, place tossed tomatoes in the oven, keeping just the pilot on, overnight.

PREPARE SUMMER TRUFFLE JAM

Place summer truffles, black truffle juice, honey, lemon juice, salt and truffle oil in a food processor. Puree until smooth. Place in a small saucepot and bring to a simmer over medium-high heat. Add apple pectin and cook gently for 5 to 8 minutes. Remove from heat and let cool. Refrigerate for 4 hours.

SIMMER OCTOPUS

Place water, wine, lemons, salt, vinegar and bay leaves in a medium-size pot and bring to a boil. Add wine corks. Lower heat to a simmer and add octopus. Cook for 25 to 35 minutes, depending on size of the octopus, until tender. Let cool by adding ice to the pot.

PREPARE CRUSTACEAN SAUCE

Sauté oil, onions, garlic, celery and bell pepper in a stockpot over medium-high heat. Sweat until onions are translucent, about 8 minutes. Add shrimp and lobster bodies and sauté for 3 minutes. Add tomato paste, roasted tomato, thyme and bay leaves. Cook until tomato paste starts to stick to the bottom of the pan, about 5 minutes. Deglaze with wine. Add stock, Pernod, Worcestershire, salt and pepper. Bring to a gentle boil and reduce to one-third. Strain through a fine-mesh sieve into a large saucepot and return to heat, again reducing by one-third. Add cream and brandy. Reduce for 20 minutes or until sauce reaches a consistency that will coat the back of a spoon.

PREPARE SMOKED POTATO

Cook baby potatoes in a steamer for 18 minutes. Allow to cool and slice into ½-inch rounds. Place in a deep-bottomed pan and seal with plastic wrap. Prepare a Smoking Gun, or a traditional smoker, loading wood chips per the manufacturer's directions. Smoke potatoes 2 to 3 times to enhance the flavor, 15 to 20 minutes. Place oil and butter in a sauté pan over medium heat. Add potato slices and cook for 2 minutes on each side or until they reach a golden crisp. Season with salt and pepper.

SEAR OCTOPUS

Slice tentacles into 2½- to 3-inch strips. Toss in olive oil, salt and pepper. Place octopus in a sauté pan over high heat. Press down on octopus with a spatula while sautéing until a golden color is achieved, about 3 minutes. Flip and repeat on the other side. Remove from pan.

ASSEMBLE

Arrange crustacean sauce on each plate. Add raisin tomato, smoked potato, seared octopus and truffle jelly. Finish with truffle oil and thyme on top.

MAZARA DEL VALLO PRAWNS IN ORANGE SAUCE WITH SALMON ROE AND FRENCH BEANS

My favorite prawns come from Mazara del Vallo, a small port in Sicily. They are deep red and sweet like honey. Of course, you can substitute any good quality prawn. But remember, just like Louisiana crawfish, one of the best parts is when you suck the heads.

Serves 6

ORANGE SAUCE

2 quarts freshly squeezed orange juice
1 tablespoon grapeseed oil
½ cup extra-virgin olive oil
Pinch of sea salt

PRAWNS

6 cups water
Pinch of sea salt
2 tablespoons white wine vinegar
2 sprigs fresh thyme
2 bay leaves
2 lemons, halved
6 prawns, heads and tails on, peeled and deveined

FRENCH BEANS

½ pound French beans, stems removed
1 tablespoon extra-virgin olive oil
Sea salt, to taste
Freshly ground black pepper, to taste
½ teaspoon fresh mint, finely chopped

FOR ASSEMBLY

2 ounces salmon roe
½ cup fresh chives, chopped
1 red bell pepper, cut into brunoise
2 tablespoons extra-virgin olive oil
Sea salt, to taste
Freshly ground black pepper, to taste

PREPARE ORANGE SAUCE

Strain orange juice through a fine-mesh sieve to remove pulp. In a wide saucepan, reduce to a consistency that will coat the back of a spoon. Remove from heat and place in a blender. With blender running, add oils and salt a little at a time.

PREPARE PRAWNS

In a medium saucepot, place water, salt, vinegar, thyme, bay leaves and lemons. Bring to a hard boil, add prawns and cook for 2 to 3 minutes, depending on size, until cooked through. Reserve for plating.

PREPARE BEANS

Bring pot of water to a boil and prepare an ice bath. Blanch beans for 3 to 3½ minutes. Drain beans and chill in ice bath. Remove, drain and towel dry. Halve vertically. Toss in oil, salt, pepper and mint.

ASSEMBLE

Sauce 6 plates and top with 2 prawns each. Nest green beans to the side. Place salmon roe around outside. Finish with chives, bell pepper, oil, salt and pepper.

SALADS

THE APPETITE BOOSTER

Let Flavors and Textures Speak

I think salad is like a nice sorbet. It cleanses your palate and gives you a quick appetite boost, preparing you for the next dish, the same way an appetizer should.

If you are going to make a salad, it is crucial to make a good salad. It should be simple and use the best available greens, free of pesticides. If you are not buying organic lettuces, make sure to remove and discard the outer leaves, which will be the most affected by chemicals.

I like the more full-bodied greens, like romaine, radicchio and endive. Kale has also become one of my new favorites. With rigid greens like these, you should wash them in ice-cold water to keep them nice and crisp. They will stand up to tossing, but use a light vinaigrette.

For more delicate greens, such as arugula, use a light touch by drizzling your dressing instead of tossing. I love the very small leaves of arugula because you taste more of that bitter bite. To offset the bitter, I pair the greens with something sweet—and same goes for radicchio. Strawberries and radicchio are wonderful together. Or you can dress the bitter lettuces with a vinaigrette sweetened with orange juice or honey. The type of vinegar you use can give your vinaigrette more character. Experiment with champagne vinegar, different types of balsamic and flavored vinegars such as raspberry.

Not all salads require greens, as you will discover in this section where I've developed recipes that use fennel, peaches, beets and tomatoes as the centerpieces, rather than your typical lettuces.

Like everything you bring to the table, let the natural flavors and textures of your salad speak for themselves. You and your guests will love what they have to say.

ENDIVE AND FRISÉE POPCORN SALAD WITH ROASTED PEAR, PIAVE CHEESE AND BLACK TRUFFLE

I love this combination of popcorn and truffles—something so simple with something so indulgent. I prefer Piave, a cheese named for a river in northern Italy, but a good Parmigiano-Reggiano works well, too.

Serves 6

PEARS

3 Roasted Pears (page 212)

VINAIGRETTE

1 tablespoon honey
2 teaspoons poaching liquid from Roasted Pears (see above)
1 teaspoon red wine vinegar
2½ teaspoons lemon juice
½ cup black truffle oil

SALAD

5 ounces endive, cut into ½-inch pieces
2 ounces frisée, stems discarded, cut into small pieces
2 cups popcorn
1 ounce black truffle, thinly sliced
4 ounces Piave cheese, shaved

PREPARE PEARS

Set aside the liquid.

PREPARE VINAIGRETTE

In a medium mixing bowl, combine honey, roasted pear liquid, vinegar and lemon juice. Whisk in the black truffle oil, adding small amounts slowly to keep dressing emulsified.

PREPARE SALAD AND ASSEMBLE

Toss endive, frisée and vinaigrette in medium mixing bowl. Divide salad among 6 plates. Top with popcorn, black truffle slices and cheese. Cut pear halves in ¼-inch slices, leaving intact at small end. Fan slices on side of plate.

HONEYED BEET AND PEACH SALAD WITH WHIPPED GOAT CHEESE, SUNFLOWER SEED PRALINE AND RASPBERRY VINAIGRETTE

This makes a dazzling, multidimensional first course. You can prepare most everything ahead of time and then bring it all together at the last minute.

Serves 6

BEETS
18 baby red beets
1 tablespoon honey
1 cup water, room temperature

SUNFLOWER SEED PRALINE
2 egg whites
¼ cup sugar
1 vanilla bean
¼ teaspoon cinnamon
1 cup unsalted sunflower seeds

WHIPPED GOAT CHEESE
6 ounces goat cheese
¼ cup sour cream
¼ cup mascarpone cheese
2 tablespoons heavy cream

RASPBERRY VINAIGRETTE
2 tablespoons raspberry vinegar
2 tablespoons champagne vinegar
¼ cup red beet juice
¼ cup Raspberry Juice (page 208)
2 tablespoons honey
1 cup grapeseed oil
Pinch of salt
Pinch freshly ground black pepper

SALAD
5 peaches
2 tablespoons olive oil
Salt, to taste
Pinch freshly ground black pepper

PREPARE BEETS
Wash beets thoroughly and cut off greens, leaving 1 inch of stem. If sous vide equipment is available, place beets, honey and water in Cryovac bag and seal. Sous vide for 25 minutes at 175°F. Alternately, preheat oven to 400°F. Wrap beets (without honey) individually in foil and roast for 25 minutes until tender through center. Or, place beets in a medium pot, then add honey and enough water to cover. Bring to a boil and cook until tender, approximately 25 minutes. With any method, while beets cook place ice in a bowl of cold water to cool. Place cooked beets in ice bath. When cool, peel using a towel. Cut beets in half.

PREPARE SUNFLOWER SEED PRALINE
Preheat oven to 350°F. In a small mixing bowl, whip egg whites and sugar to a soft peak. Split vanilla bean in half and scrape to remove paste. Add paste and cinnamon to egg white mixture. Toss in sunflower seeds. On a sheet tray lined with parchment paper, spread mixture as thinly and evenly as possible. Bake until golden brown, about 5 minutes. Let cool, then break into pieces. Store unused portions in airtight plastic bag or container.

PREPARE WHIPPED GOAT CHEESE
Using an electric mixer, place goat cheese, sour cream and mascarpone into a medium bowl. Mix on low speed for 1 minute, adding cream as needed to loosen the mixture. Whip only until mixed and soft; mascarpone will separate if over-whipped.

PREPARE VINAIGRETTE
In a small mixing bowl, combine vinegars, beet juice, raspberry juice and honey. While whisking the mixture slowly, add grapeseed oil to emulsify. Add salt and pepper.

ASSEMBLE
Cut peaches in half, remove pits and plunge into boiling water for 10 seconds. Remove skins by rubbing with paper towel. Cut into slices. In a large mixing bowl, toss beets and peaches in olive oil, salt and pepper. Arrange among 6 plates alternating beets and peach slices. Place a dollop of whipped goat cheese in center. Drizzle salad with vinaigrette and sprinkle praline on top to finish.

TREVISO RADICCHIO AND STRAWBERRY WITH GORGONZOLA PISTACHIO TRUFFLES

Radicchio can be bitter for some palates, but the strawberries help mellow that. And the truffles are a flavor bomb of cheesy goodness.

Serves 6

GORGONZOLA TRUFFLES

2 ounces gorgonzola dolce
2 ounces mascarpone
6 dates, pitted and diced
1 cup pistachio flour (or dust)

BALSAMIC-ORANGE REDUCTION

½ cup freshly squeezed orange juice
1 cup balsamic vinegar
2 tablespoons sugar

SALAD

6 radicchio di Treviso
1 pint strawberries
2 tablespoons extra-virgin olive oil
2 tablespoons balsamic-orange reduction
Pinch of sea salt
Pinch of freshly ground black pepper

PREPARE GORGONZOLA TRUFFLES

In a stand mixer, using paddle attachment, combine gorgonzola, mascarpone and dates. Shape into ¼-inch balls and roll into pistachio flour or dust. (If you cannot find pistachio flour or dust, make your own by processing 1 cup whole, unsalted pistachios in a food processor to a fine consistency. If it clumps, add 1 tablespoon of flour.)

PREPARE BALSAMIC-ORANGE REDUCTION

Strain orange juice to remove pulp. In a saucepan over medium-high heat, combine orange juice, vinegar and sugar. Stir occasionally while watching closely to prevent from boiling over. Reduce by 30 percent to 1 cup of liquid. Chill in refrigerator.

PREPARE SALAD

Cut the lettuce heads lengthwise and slice strawberries. Place all in a mixing bowl. Add olive oil, balsamic-orange reduction, salt and pepper; toss gently. Divide the salad among 6 plates. Garnish each plate with 3 gorgonzola truffles. Drizzle with balsamic orange-reduction.

DECONSTRUCTED TOMATOES WITH BALSAMIC JELLY AND LIQUID BUFFALO MOZZARELLA

When an excellent tomato meets buffalo mozzarella, it's a wonderful thing. Here, we take the mozzarella back to its origins by melting it in its own water. Then you can shoot it out of its tomato bowl with the balsamic jelly—familiar flavors exciting the mouth in a brand-new way.

Serves 6

BALSAMIC JELLY

1 cup balsamic vinegar
2 tablespoons sugar
Zest of 3 lemons
Zest of 3 oranges
Pinch of sea salt
1 teaspoon agar

LIQUID MOZZARELLA

8 ounces buffalo mozzarella
⅔ cup buffalo mozzarella water
1 cup heavy cream
Sea salt, to taste

TOMATO AND GARNISH

9 Campari tomatoes
Fresh micro basil
Sea salt, to taste
Freshly ground black pepper, to taste
¼ cup extra-virgin olive oil

PREPARE BALSAMIC JELLY

In a small saucepan, bring balsamic, sugar, lemon and orange zests and salt to a boil. Reduce for a few minutes. Whisk in agar and cook until mixture starts to thicken, about 30 seconds. Pour onto a baking sheet. Let cool completely. Using a turner spatula, transfer jelly to a cutting board (don't worry if jelly breaks into pieces). Cut into small brunoise. Reserve for plating.

PREPARE LIQUID MOZZARELLA

In small saucepan, combine mozzarella, mozzarella water, cream and salt and bring to a boil. Lower heat to a soft boil. Reduce mixture until dissolved. Let cool before plating.

ASSEMBLE

Remove stems from tomatoes. Cut in half and remove cores with a melon baller or spoon, creating bowls, being careful not to break outer skins. Place 3 tomato halves on each plate. Place about ½ teaspoon balsamic jelly into each tomato and top with liquid mozzarella. Garnish with basil. Season with salt and pepper and drizzle with oil.

CRAZY BUBBLING TOMATO WITH BURRATINA AND GREEN PEA SHOOTS

This is another variation on the tomato-meets-mozzarella theme because Burratina is a creamy type of mozzarella. You'll understand why we call it crazy when you see the tomato juice flowing over the cheese like lava from a volcano.

Serves 6

CRAZY BUBBLING TOMATO

1¼ cups tomato juice
1 cup, plus 2 tablespoons whole milk
Sea salt, to taste
Pinch of freshly ground black pepper
1 teaspoon xanthan gum
2 tablespoons Versawhip

LIQUID BASIL

¼ cup clear vegetable broth
2 ounces basil leaves
1 ounce spinach
1 tablespoon extra-virgin olive oil
Sea salt, to taste
Pinch of freshly ground black pepper
½ teaspoon xanthan gum

BURRATINA

12 ounces Burratina cheese
2 ounces pea shoots
½ pound dry ice
Water, if needed
Sea salt, to taste
Pinch of freshly ground pepper
3 tablespoons extra-virgin olive oil

PREPARE CRAZY TOMATO

Combine tomato juice, milk, salt and pepper in a measuring pitcher. Whisk in xanthan gum and Versawhip until smooth.

PREPARE LIQUID BASIL

Bring all ingredients to room temperature and place in a blender. Puree and pass through a fine-mesh sieve.

ASSEMBLE

Place Burratina in the center of a plate and place pea shoots next to cheese. Garnish plate with liquid basil. Using gloves, place small chips of dry ice in an espresso cup. Pour tomato dressing into espresso cup, fully submerging the dry ice and allowing dressing to bubble out of the cup, over the Burratina. Add water, as necessary, to activate more bubbles. When a sufficient amount of bubbles have developed, spoon them over cheese and remove cup from plate. Season with salt and pepper and drizzle olive oil around the plate.

**Note: Dry ice is extremely cold and can cause frostbite. Always use leather gloves or a kitchen towel when handling dry ice.*

FENNEL AND ORANGE WITH PICKLED RED ONIONS AND BLACK SAMBUCA DRESSING

This refreshing salad provides a double dose of anise—from the fennel and the dressing. The lemon juice tempers everything and brings out the sweetness.

Serves 6

BLACK SAMBUCA DRESSING

1 cup black sambuca
¼ cup grapeseed oil
1 tablespoon extra-virgin olive oil
1 teaspoon lemon juice
Pinch of sea salt

FENNEL AND ORANGE SALAD

3 fennel bulbs
3 oranges, peeled
Pinch of sea salt
1 teaspoon pink peppercorns, divided
3 tablespoons extra-virgin olive oil
1 teaspoon lemon juice
½ to 1 cup Pickled Red Onions (page 211)
6 teaspoons Orange Nectar (page 210)
30 small leaves fresh mint
18 small sprigs fresh dill

PREPARE BLACK SAMBUCA DRESSING

In a medium saucepan over medium heat, reduce sambuca by 30 percent. Remove from heat and let cool for a few minutes. Whisk in oils, a little at a time, to emulsify. Stir in lemon juice and salt and let rest.

PREPARE SALAD

Shave fennel bulbs into thin slices using a mandoline. Segment oranges. Toss in mixing bowl with salt, ½ teaspoon peppercorns, oil and lemon juice. Add pickled red onions, stir and divide among 6 plates. Drizzle black sambuca dressing and orange nectar around the plate. Finish with remaining peppercorns, and garnish with mint and dill.

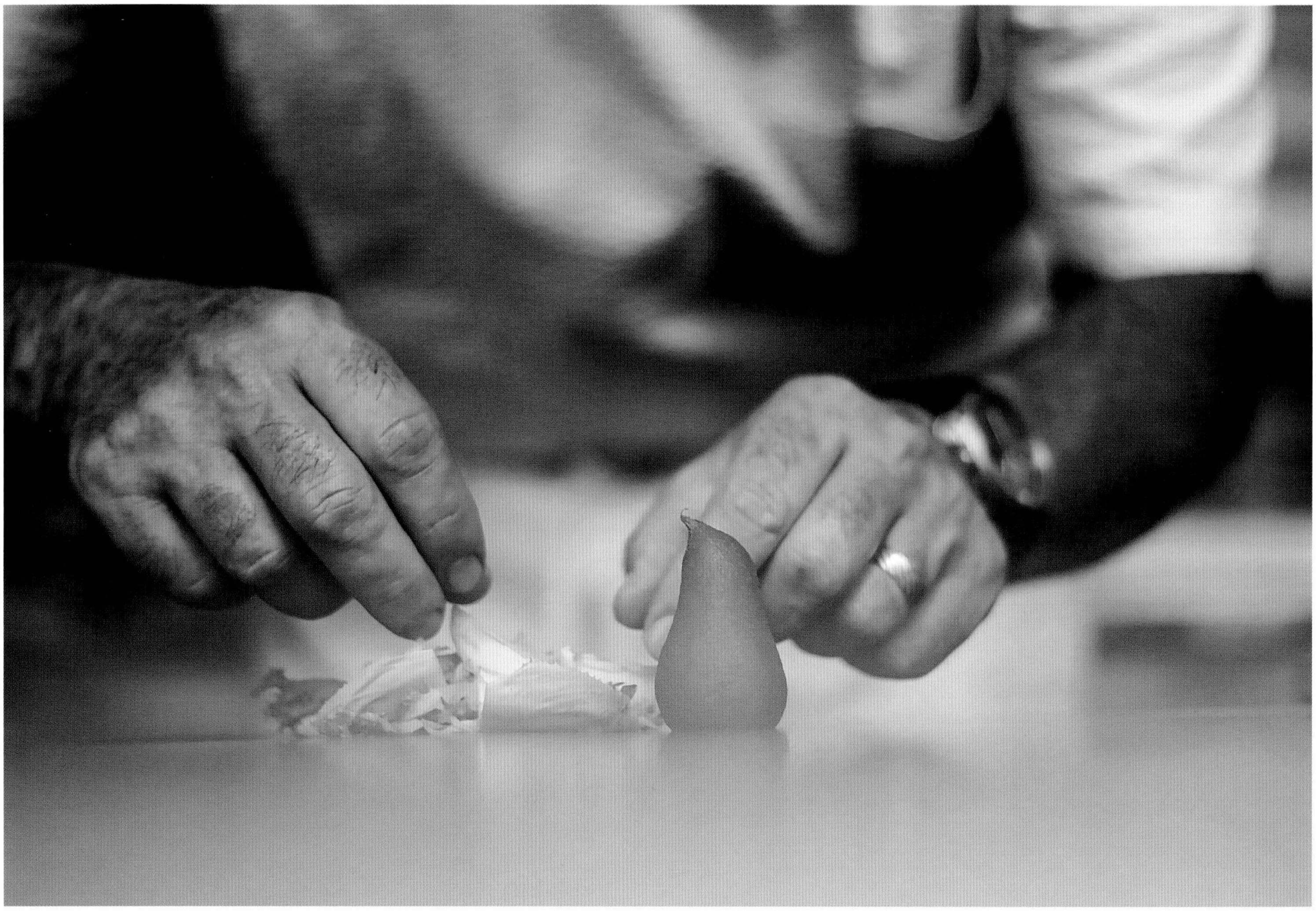

EVOLUTION OF CAESAR SALAD

It's funny, everything in a Caesar salad is Italian, but the Caesar salad is American. When I first tried it here, back when everyone was doing it tableside, I absolutely loved it. Then everybody was doing it and it started to declass it. In every step of this evolution, 90 percent of the ingredients I use are the same. Put them all together and you get entirely different textures. Which is best? It depends on the person, the mood, the moment.

LIQUID CAESAR SALAD
4 ounces Parmesan, small chunks
3 cloves garlic
3 egg yolks
14 fillets canned anchovies
1½ tablespoons Dijon mustard
1 pound romaine lettuce, torn into pieces
12 leaves spinach
½ cup extra-virgin olive oil
¼ cup lemon juice
2 tablespoons red wine vinegar
1 cup vegetable broth
Sea salt, to taste
Pinch of freshly ground black pepper

CAESAR DRESSING
8 fillets canned anchovies
1 teaspoon garlic, minced
2 egg yolks
1 tablespoon lemon juice
1 teaspoon sherry vinegar
1 tablespoon Dijon mustard
¼ teaspoon sea salt
Pinch of freshly ground black pepper
5 tablespoons extra-virgin olive oil
5 tablespoons grapeseed oil

CAESAR ROLL
3½ ounces romaine lettuce
1 piece soy wrap
2 tablespoons Caesar Dressing (see above)
2 ounces Parmesan cheese, shaved

SOFT CAESAR GELATO
1 egg yolk
1 teaspoon mustard powder
1 teaspoon garlic powder
1 tablespoon olive oil
½ tablespoon lemon juice
3 anchovy fillets, minced
¼ cup Parmesan cheese, microplaned
1 cup Greek yogurt
½ tablespoon red wine vinegar

SETTING BATH
4 cups water
2½ teaspoons calcium chloride

TOMATO CAVIAR
½ cup Tomato Water (page 212)
¾ teaspoon sodium alginate
½ cup tomato juice

FOR ASSEMBLY
Olive oil
Freshly ground black pepper, to taste

PREPARE LIQUID CAESAR SALAD
In a blender, place Parmesan, garlic, egg yolks, anchovies, mustard, lettuce, spinach, oil, lemon juice, vinegar and broth. Puree on high, then season to taste. Pour into shot glasses.

PREPARE CAESAR DRESSING
In a mixing bowl, combine anchovies, garlic, egg yolks, lemon juice, vinegar, mustard, salt and pepper. Mix using an immersion blender. Blend slowly, adding oils a little at a time to ensure dressing is fully emulsified. Store dressing in an airtight container for up to 1 week.

PREPARE CAESAR ROLL
Chiffonade lettuce. Line a bamboo rolling mat with plastic wrap. Lay soy wrap on top. On one end, make a bed of the lettuce strips the width of the soy wrap. Coat lettuce with Caesar dressing and top with cheese. Wet your fingertips and one end of the soy sheet to ensure that it will make a seal. Starting on the dry end, roll tightly, making sure plastic wrap doesn't get wrapped into the roll. Cut into 4 pieces. Top with tomato caviar as garnish.

PREPARE SOFT CAESAR GELATO
Combine all ingredients in a food processor and puree. Transfer to a mixing bowl and submerge in an ice bath. Whisk for a few minutes, then refrigerate.

PREPARE SETTING BATH
Place ingredients in a large bowl and mix until dissolved.

PREPARE TOMATO CAVIAR
Blend tomato water on low speed. A vortex will form in the center of the liquid. Add sodium alginate and mix until thickened. Add tomato juice and pass through a fine-mesh sieve. Place liquid into a squeeze bottle and slowly add droplets to setting bath. Let stand for 2 to 3 minutes. Strain and rinse.

ASSEMBLE
Place 1 Caesar roll in the center of each plate and top with a small scoop tomato caviar. Add 1 quenelle gelato and 1 shot glass liquid Caesar. Drizzle with oil and pepper.

KALE, PERSIMMON AND POMEGRANATE WITH OLIVE OIL EMULSION AND CHAMPAGNE VINEGAR GELÉE

Kale is now in high demand and is so good for you nutritionally. Here, I envisioned greens you would eat in the winter, so I created, in a salad version, kale with wintery fruits and color.

Serves 6

CHAMPAGNE VINEGAR GELÉE

⅛ cup white balsamic vinegar
½ cup champagne vinegar
½ cup sugar
1 cup water
Pinch of salt
3 sheets gelatin

OLIVE OIL EMULSION

2 tablespoons lemon juice
3 egg yolks
1 cup extra-virgin olive oil
¼ teaspoon salt

KALE SALAD

18 spears asparagus, trimmed
½ pound kale, washed, stemmed and chopped
2 persimmons, sliced
½ cup pomegranate seeds
⅛ cup extra-virgin olive oil
1 tablespoon lemon juice
Salt, to taste
Freshly ground black pepper, to taste

PREPARE CHAMPAGNE VINEGAR GELÉE

Simmer vinegars, sugar, water and salt in a small saucepot for 15 minutes. Remove from heat. In a separate container, add 2 cups tepid water to gelatin sheets. Allow gelatin to soften, then remove and squeeze out excess water. Add gelatin sheets to saucepot and whisk for 1 minute. Place mixture in a 6 x 6-inch container. Refrigerate for 4 hours.

PREPARE OLIVE OIL EMULSION

Place lemon juice and egg yolks in a food processor and puree for 1 minute. With processor running, slowly add olive oil in a thin stream, no thicker than a piece of string, until all oil is incorporated. Add salt and set aside.

PREPARE KALE SALAD

To prepare asparagus, boil salted water in a large pot. Meanwhile, prepare an ice bath. Blanch asparagus in boiling water for 3 minutes or until tender. Chill rapidly in an ice bath for about 2 minutes, then remove and pat dry with towels. Set aside. Combine chopped kale, persimmons, pomegranate seeds, oil, lemon juice, salt and pepper in a large bowl. Mix to dress the kale.

ASSEMBLE

Divide salad among 6 plates. Smash champagne vinegar gelée and scatter over the salad. Finish each plate with the olive oil emulsion.

MICROGREENS

Farm. Fresh. Sweet!

Let me tell you a story about Ken Ryan, gentleman farmer for more than 30 years. He once brought us some Everglades tomatoes—tiny, about the size of blueberries. They were the sweetest tomatoes ever. We said, "Bring more!" He told us the birds liked them, too. He couldn't always bring them to us because he only grew so many.

Those are two reasons why Ken's Herban Gardens in North Fort Myers is the best and one of our top produce purveyors: he lets things grow naturally, and he only does what he loves.

Here's a guy who made a name for himself in New England delivering farm produce in his truck to restaurants, like in the old days.

He told me, "Fabrizio, I grow it, I harvest it and I deliver it. I'm like a mobile farmers' market." And that's the truth. Every Thursday he shows up with surprises. He begins his deliveries in Naples, so we get early pickings. He brings up to 50 varieties of produce some days. It can be different every week, but we have an understanding. He knows what I like—whatever is unique and exquisitely flavorful.

Like the Everglades tomatoes. Like these tiny, oh-so-sweet peppers he once brought. We begged for more of them, too. But he only grows small batches. He grows around 80 varieties of microgreens, herbs, vegetables and fruits each winter season, but not in great volume. That's what makes his produce so special.

We especially love his microgreens but we also buy herbs and vegetables from him. The wonderful thing about his produce? It was harvested just the day before or the morning of delivery. Unlike the big operations that ship from overseas, it truly is fresh, meaning it has a longer shelf life in the restaurant.

Ken nurses his plants like babies, so they are really beautiful when they arrive at our back door. I call him a "custom-made magician" where flavor is concerned. We work very closely, making suggestions and telling him what we are looking for in a certain product.

Ken is what I call a boutique farmer. He's very particular and believes in farming the old-fashioned way—naturally and always in real dirt. He gets up at 3 a.m. He doesn't work on computers or cell phones, as he'd rather be talking to his plants than talking on the phone. He is a real foodie and very particular with which chefs he will supply because he wants his precious plants showcased in the best possible way.

SOUPS

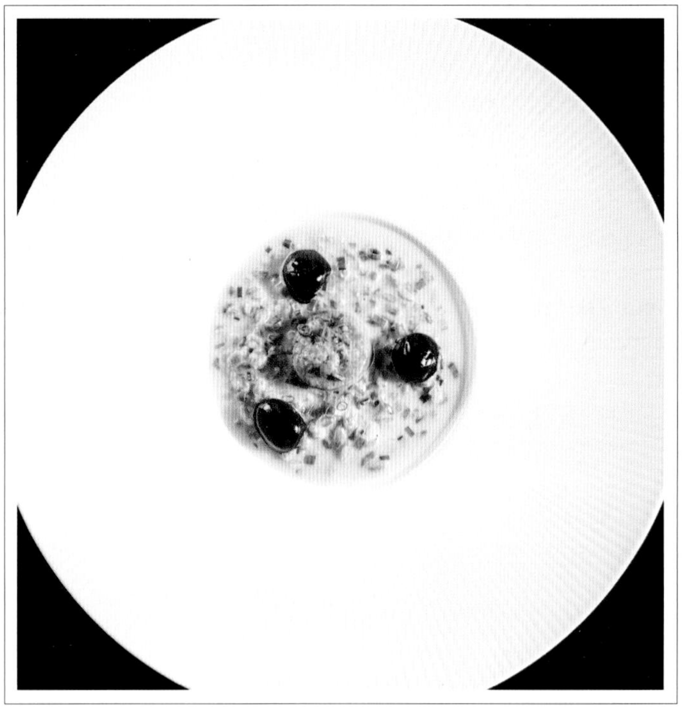

SUPER BOWLS

A Game of Common Sense

‡

Soup too often gets bullied and belittled. That's because home cooks sometimes make soup to clean out the refrigerator and use up what's in the cupboard. In Italy, when we see someone making a dish with too many ingredients in it, we ask: "What are you doing, making a soup?" It has derogatory connotations.

For a good soup, you must plan carefully so that the ingredients work together and complement each other, bringing out their best elements. You must ask: "What can I do to make the flavors taste wonderful together?"

The most important ingredient is common sense. The more you cook meat, the more flavor it adds to the soup. That's not always true of vegetables. Take green peas, for example. Overcooking kills the flavor. That's why in my pea soup, I use some fresh peas in the soup while it's cooking and then I add more fresh peas to the blender for the puree.

With other dishes, I can generally tell by sight, smell and touch if they have enough salt and pepper or are cooked to the proper doneness. But soup is one of the few things I actually need to taste to know it is right, to make sure it has cooked enough to have good flavor but not so much that the flavor is too concentrated.

The secret to a good soup is starting with homemade stock. Do not skip this step. You cannot just put meat into a soup and expect it to do all the work. If you taste a piece of meat and then drink a shot of meat stock, you will see, the flavors are entirely different. The secret is in the bones—that's where all the flavor is—and that's what you need to make the stocks and glacés you will find in the Pantry section at the back of the book.

Soup is so much more than leftovers. It's an orchestrated dance of flavors. Starting a meal with soup is one more way of warming up your guests for the meal's crescendo.

WATERMELON GAZPACHO WITH GUANICALE, FETA AND ARUGULA SORBET

Watermelon and arugula salads are justly popular, but sometimes here in Florida they can wind up just a little too warm. Turning the watermelon into gazpacho and the arugula into sorbet solves that problem in a refreshing way.

Serves 6

SORBET

2¼ cups water
¾ cup glucose (or white sugar)
5 ounces arugula
2 egg whites
½ tablespoon lemon juice
1 teaspoon extra-virgin olive oil
Pinch of sea salt

GAZPACHO

4 cups (about 2 pounds) seedless watermelon, cubed
1 jalapeño, seeded, membranes removed and diced
1 cup (1 small) roasted red beet, cubed
1 cup cucumber, peeled, seeded and cubed
¾ cup celery, chopped
1 tablespoon lemon juice
1 tablespoon lime juice
1 tablespoon cilantro, chopped
½ tablespoon Tabasco sauce
2 tablespoons honey
2 tablespoons extra-virgin olive oil
2 tablespoons red wine vinegar
½ teaspoon sea salt
½ teaspoon freshly ground black pepper

FOR ASSEMBLY

¼ cup crumbled feta cheese
3 ounces guanciale or pancetta, sliced paper thin and julienned
Chives, chopped
Fresh dill sprigs

PREPARE SORBET

Bring water and glucose to a boil in a small saucepot, then chill in an ice bath. Combine with arugula and puree in a blender. Pass through a fine-mesh sieve, discarding pulp. Combine mixture with egg whites, lemon juice, oil and salt. Process in an ice-cream maker and freeze. Remove 5 to 7 minutes before scooping.

PREPARE GAZPACHO

Place all ingredients in a blender and puree.

ASSEMBLE

Divide soup among 6 bowls. Sprinkle with feta cheese and top with guanciale. To finish, top gazpacho with a dollop of sorbet and garnish with chives and dill.

MUSSELS AND BRUSSELS WITH DUCK WING BROTH

Wings and mussels are popular foods, but they are messy and can be difficult to eat. I wanted to bring the two together so that guests could enjoy them without working too hard or staining their clothes. The duck wing broth offers much more flavor than chicken, and it coaxes out something unexpected from the mussels. As for the Brussels sprouts? Well, that's the surprise.

Serves 6

DUCK WINGS

8 duck wings
1 tablespoon extra-virgin olive oil
Salt, to taste
Freshly ground black pepper, to taste

MUSSELS SOUP

4 tablespoons extra-virgin olive oil, divided
5 cloves garlic, sliced, divided
4 pounds mussels, scrubbed
1 small shallot, thinly sliced
6 Brussels sprouts, shaved on a mandoline
Pinch of sea salt
Pinch of freshly ground black pepper
2 quarts Duck Wing Stock (page 209)
1 teaspoon colatura anchovy sauce (or Asian fish sauce)

FOR ASSEMBLY

1 tablespoon Italian parsley, chopped
½ cup green onion, diagonal cuts

PREPARE DUCK WINGS

Preheat oven to 375°F. In a mixing bowl, combine all ingredients. Lay wings on a baking sheet, transfer to the oven and cook for 30 minutes. Let cool, then remove meat and set aside, discarding skins.

PREPARE MUSSELS AND BROTH

In a large, wide sauté pan, place 2 tablespoons oil, half the sliced garlic and the mussels. Cook over high heat until mussels open. Remove mussels from pan and set aside to cool. Pick meat from shells.

In a small saucepan, place remaining oil and garlic and the shallot slices. Sweat shallots until translucent, 2 to 3 minutes. Add Brussels sprouts, reserved duck meat, salt and pepper and cook for 2 minutes. Add stock and anchovy sauce and bring to a gentle boil, cooking for 3 to 4 minutes.

ASSEMBLE

Divide shelled mussels among 6 soup bowls. Pour broth over top and finish with parsley and green onion.

SMOKED CHERRY SOUP WITH FARRO AND WILD BOAR SAUSAGE

I created this dish one night for my Chef's Table, and it immediately garnered rave reviews. If you can't source wild boar sausage, no problem, you can substitute another sausage. It's the smoked cherry that brings it all together and adds an earthy sweetness.

Serves 6

FARRO

3 cups farro
4 cups water

SMOKED CHERRIES

1 cup dried cherries
1 cup crème de cassis
¼ cup cherry wood chips

SOUP

2 tablespoons extra-virgin olive oil
¼ cup celery, finely diced
¼ cup onion, finely diced
¼ cup carrots, finely diced
1 tablespoon fresh rosemary, chopped
1 tablespoon fresh sage, chopped
3 cups farro
8 cups Chicken Stock (page 209)
½ pound wild boar sausage, links whole
1 tablespoon chives, chopped
1 teaspoon salt
1 teaspoon freshly ground black pepper

PREPARE CHERRIES AND FARRO

Soak farro in water and refrigerate overnight. Soak dried cherries in crème de cassis overnight. The next day, drain farro and cherries and discard liquid. Rinse farro under cold water and set aside. To smoke cherries, place on a tray if using a smoker, or in a container covered with plastic wrap if using a Smoking Gun. (Follow manufacturer's instructions for loading wood chips and for smoking procedure.) Smoke 2 or 3 times, until cherries retain heavy smoke flavor. Reserve for plating.

PREPARE SOUP

In a large sauté pan over medium-high heat, place oil, celery, onion, carrots, rosemary and sage, and cook until translucent, about 5 minutes. Add farro and cook for 3 minutes. Add stock and bring to a light boil, cooking for 10 minutes. Add sausage and cook for 30 to 35 minutes, then remove sausage and cut into ½-inch-thick coins. Sprinkle with chives and season to taste.

ASSEMBLE

Divide soup among 6 soup bowls. Top soup with sausage and smoked cherries.

CHICKEN VELOUTÉ WITH ROSEMARY BRIOCHE AND CARDOON SPREAD

This soup is like liquid chicken, with the different elements and flavors concentrated into easy spoonfuls. The cardoons, a tasty artichoke-like thistle, make a refined spread and wonderful dipping component.

Serves 8

BRAISED CARDOONS

2 pounds cardoons, chopped
2–3 cups Chicken Stock (page 209)
6 lemons, halved
1 tablespoon salt
1 tablespoon freshly ground black pepper
¼ cup garlic cloves

CHICKEN VELOUTÉ

⅛ cup olive oil
1 cup celery, chopped
1 cup onion, chopped
1 cup carrot, chopped
⅛ cup ginger, grated
1 tablespoon thyme, finely chopped
1 tablespoon rosemary, finely chopped
2 potatoes, peeled and chopped
2 pounds ground chicken, white meat
3 bay leaves
1 tablespoon curry powder
½ cup white wine
8 cups Chicken Stock (page 209)
1 cup Crème Fraîche (page 209)
2 tablespoons sherry
Salt, to taste
White pepper, to taste

CARDOON SPREAD

1 tablespoon lemon juice
Pinch of salt
Pinch of freshly ground black pepper
1 tablespoon extra-virgin olive oil
1 cup cream cheese
Brioche

BRAISE CARDOONS

Combine all ingredients in a large roasting pan. Cover with aluminum foil and roast at 375°F for 1 to 1½ hours, until tender. Refrigerate in its own juices. Drain, discarding liquid.

PREPARE CHICKEN VELOUTÉ

Sauté oil, celery, onion, carrot, ginger, thyme, rosemary and potatoes in a large stockpot over medium-high heat for 5 minutes or until vegetables soften. Add chicken, bay leaves and curry and cook for 10 minutes. Deglaze pan with wine and let liquid be absorbed for a few minutes. Add stock and cook for 20 to 30 minutes, until potatoes are soft. Remove bay leaves and warm a second large stockpot. Working in batches, transfer mixture to a blender, purée until smooth and pass through a fine-mesh sieve into the second pot. Add crème fraîche, sherry, salt and pepper and return to a boil, cooking for 5 minutes.

PREPARE CARDOON SPREAD

Purée braised cardoons in a food processor for 2 minutes. Pass through a sieve and return to the food processor. Add lemon juice, salt, pepper, oil and cream cheese and purée for 1 minute.

ASSEMBLE

Divide soup among 8 bowls. Place a slice of toasted brioche in the center of each bowl. Make quenelles of cardoon spread on top of each brioche. Pour soup on top to finish.

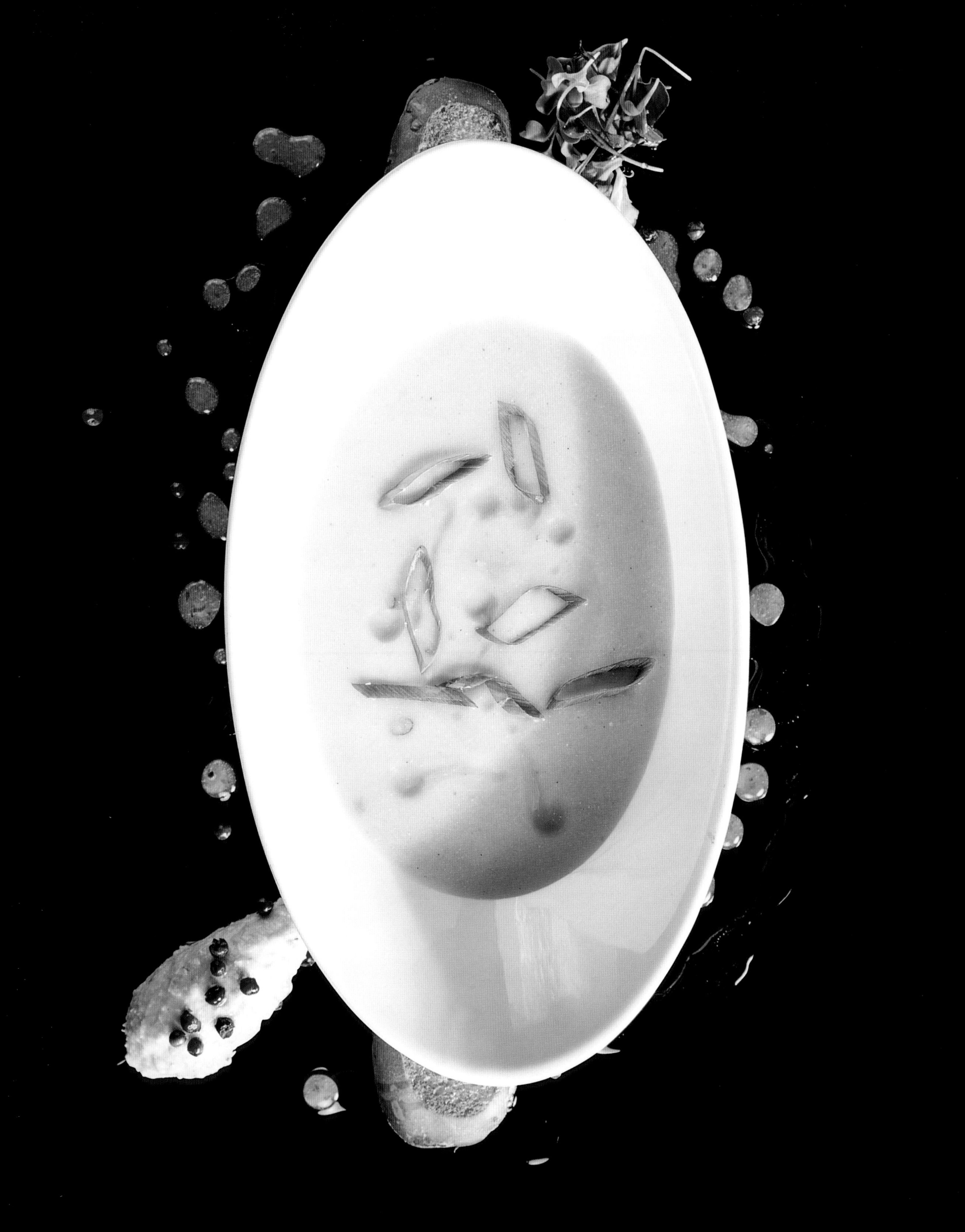

POTATO AND LEEK SOUP WITH CRÈME FRAÎCHE, CAVIAR AND QUAIL EGG

Here we take a wonderful comfort food and elevate it from rustic to elegant with caviar and quail egg. The little touch of prosciutto brings out earthy tones—a kiss to the caviar.

Serves 6

4 medium Yukon gold potatoes, peeled and diced
8 leeks, white stalks only, washed and diced
4 ounces prosciutto from hock or side cut, whole
¼ cup extra-virgin olive oil
Sea salt, to taste
Freshly ground black pepper, to taste
5 (5-inch) sprigs fresh thyme
3 bay leaves
1 teaspoon black peppercorns
6 quarts Chicken Stock (page 209)
1 cup Crème Fraîche (page 209)
6 quail eggs
1 ounce caviar
1 tablespoon chives, chopped

PROCEDURE

In a large stockpot, combine potatoes, leeks, prosciutto, olive oil, salt and pepper. Cook for 5 minutes over medium heat, stirring occasionally.

Use a 4 x 4-inch square of cheesecloth to create an herb sachet of thyme, bay leaves and peppercorns, securing with butcher's twine. Add to pot with stock. Bring to a boil and cook over medium-high heat for 25 to 30 minutes, until potatoes are soft.

Remove and discard sachet and prosciutto. Allow soup to cool somewhat, then transfer to a blender and puree until smooth. Return soup to the stockpot and add crème fraîche. Return to a simmer and heat for 5 minutes.

In nonstick sauté pan, lightly fry quail eggs sunny-side up. Place each egg in a bowl and divide caviar among 6 bowls, to the side of the egg. Sprinkle chives on top, and pour soup tableside.

SWEET PEA SOUP WITH ROASTED RICOTTA, SPECK AND HONEYSUCKLE

When I was a boy in Venice we would sometimes chew peas with pork skin—Italian snack food. I wanted to create a soup that recalled that memory. And why not add honeysuckle to boost the sweet, summer flavor of the peas?

Serves 6

ROASTED RICOTTA AND SPECK

4 ounces ricotta salata cheese, ¼- to ⅛-inch slices
3 ounces speck, finely diced
6 tablespoons butter, softened to room temperature
5 ounces (3 paper-thin slices) speck

SOUP

½ cup extra-virgin olive oil
½ cup sweet onion, diced
4-ounce chunk of speck, whole
1 teaspoon fresh thyme, finely chopped
4 cups fresh sweet green peas
1 quart Chicken Stock (page 209)
1 cup frozen peas
Sea salt, to taste
Freshly ground black pepper, to taste
Chives, chopped
30 pieces honeysuckle
1 ounce microgreens

PREPARE RICOTTA AND SPECK

Preheat oven to 500°F. Roast ricotta for 1 to 3 minutes, until golden brown. Remove and let cool. Lower oven to 400°F.

In a food processor, combine diced speck and butter. Whip until entirely incorporated. Take 1 slice speck and spread half speck-butter mixture on top. Repeat, layering speck and butter, then top with third slice to create a "sandwich." Cut speck sandwich into ½-inch-wide strips 5 inches long. Line a baking sheet with parchment paper, place speck strips on top, then cover with another sheet of parchment. Place a heavy skillet on top to weigh down. Bake for 3 to 5 minutes, until crispy. Remove and let cool, keeping in mind that it gets crispier as it cools.

PREPARE SOUP

In medium stockpot over medium heat, cook oil, onion, whole speck and thyme until onions are translucent. Add fresh peas and stock. Bring to a boil and cook for 8 to 15 minutes. Remove speck. Allow to cool somewhat, then transfer to a blender. Add frozen peas and blend until smooth. Return soup to a stockpot, season to taste and gently boil for a few more minutes.

ASSEMBLE

Divide soup among 6 cups, each with a diameter under 4½ inches. Sprinkle chives and place baked ricotta on top. Add 1 slice crispy speck across rim. Place honeysuckle and microgreens over crispy speck.

PASTA

ESSENTIAL INDULGENCE

The Heart of Italian Cuisine

‡

Try to think of life without pasta. Who doesn't get sad?

With the big controversies over carbs and gluten these days, some naysayers would have us thinking we should live life without pasta. But don't deny yourself. When you're in the mood for pasta, eat it as you would anything else—in moderation. We can even create a wonderful gluten-free pasta without you ever knowing it's gluten free. And if you want to avoid the guilt, skip bread or dessert. In Italy, most people eat pasta every single day. It's a big part of Italian history. It's a cultural food, and the first thing most people think of when they hear "Italian cuisine."

I honor Italy's strong tradition of pasta while trying to demonstrate a wide sphere of influences on my cooking. So, like everything that I cook in my restaurants and that I envisioned for this book, I try to take traditional flavors and food combinations that people love and reinvent them a little.

I turn tortelli upside down. I stuff cappellacci with polenta—something that's unheard of in Italy. I complement cured pork with sea urchins in my pasta carbonara. I flavor gnocchi with roasted beets, ravioli with chocolate. I ask my guests and readers to keep an open mind when reading my menus and recipes. Just because you have never eaten or made something the way I do, live a little and try it. Some of the most unlikely combinations can surprise and reward with the most incredible taste sensations. Pasta is the ultimate comfort food. But me, I like to push it a little bit out of the comfort zone. So go ahead. Indulge and be happy.

RED BEET GNOCCHI WITH HAZELNUT, SPECK AND RICOTTA SALATA

Traditionally, you use potatoes to make gnocchi, so this is a twist using beets and fresh ricotta in the dough instead. The beets and hazelnut cream add sweetness and the speck and dry ricotta are salty, so you have a lot of different flavors and textures playing off each other.

Serves 6

GNOCCHI DOUGH

½ pound red beets
1 pound 00 flour
2 pounds fresh ricotta cheese
½ cup Parmesan, grated
1 egg
2 tablespoons honey
2 pinches fresh nutmeg, grated
2 teaspoons sea salt
2 quarts water
1 tablespoon olive oil
½ tablespoon sea salt

BEET HAZELNUT CREAM

¾ cup Crème Fraîche (page 209)
2 tablespoons beet juice
1 tablespoon honey
2 tablespoons hazelnut oil

SAUCE

1½ ounces hazelnuts
¼ teaspoon hazelnut oil
Pinch sea salt
2 sticks butter
½ cup whole sage leaves, lightly packed
6 ounces speck, julienned
4 ounces ricotta salata, shaved

PREPARE GNOCCHI

Wrap beets in aluminum foil and roast at 400°F for 1 to 1½ hours, until tender enough to insert a sharp knife to middle of beet. Let cool and peel using paper towel. Puree in food processor until very finely chopped.

Strain any excess liquid from ricotta cheese through cheesecloth.

Measure ½ pound flour (about 1 cup) into a large bowl. Add ricotta, Parmesan, egg, honey, nutmeg, 2 teaspoons salt and pureed beets. Mix well with hands. Continue to knead in flour 2 tablespoons at a time. Dough should be semi-soft but elastic enough to roll with hands.

Divide dough into 6 portions and, on a floured surface, shape with hands into long rolls about the circumference of a nickel. Cut strips at an angle into ⅜-inch pieces.

Bring water, olive oil and ½ tablespoon of salt to a gentle boil in a pot. Add gnocchi pieces 2 at a time. Give a quick stir so gnocchi does not stick to bottom of pot. When gnocchi floats to surface, use a skimmer to transfer into cold water bath. Remove from cold water into colander. Continue process until all gnocchi is cooked.

The gnocchi can be made a day ahead of time. Toss with olive oil and store sealed in refrigerator. Bring to room temperature to use in recipe.

PREPARE BEET HAZELNUT CREAM

Blend crème fraîche, beet juice and honey in a bowl. Whisk in the hazelnut oil a little at a time to incorporate.

PREPARE SAUCE

Toss hazelnuts with ¼ teaspoon hazelnut oil and salt. Toast in the oven at 350°F for 12 to 15 minutes. Let cool, then coarsely chop.

Melt butter in sauté pan on medium heat. Add sage, speck and gnocchi. Cook, stirring very gently, for 2 minutes until gnocchi is heated through and lightly golden.

ASSEMBLE

Spoon hazelnut cream onto 6 plates, swirling in a fan shape at the edges. Add gnocchi and sauce. Top with dry ricotta and sprinkle with nuts.

CHAMOMILE—LANGOUSTINE RISOTTO WITH GRAPPA AND LEMON

This dish is so delicious and satisfying that you will want to take a nap with a smile on your face when you're finished eating it. To make good risotto, don't forget that rice loves attention. If you don't give rice your full focus, it will get upset. Please don't precook the rice because it will cry, and when it cries it becomes mushy.

Serves 6

CHAMOMILE CHICKEN BROTH

¾ cup fresh chamomile flowers (or 6 tablespoons dried)
1 quart Chicken Broth (page 209)

RISOTTO

3 pounds unshelled langoustines
3 tablespoons extra-virgin olive oil
1 tablespoon butter
2 shallots, finely chopped
14 ounces Acquerello Carnaroli rice
¼ cup white wine
1 pint Lobster Stock (page 210)
4 ounces (1 stick) cold butter, cut in pieces
4 ounces mascarpone cheese
1 tablespoon lemon juice
½ tablespoon chamomile grappa
1 tablespoon Italian parsley, chopped
Sea salt, to taste
White pepper, to taste
¼ cup fresh chamomile flowers

PREPARE CHAMOMILE CHICKEN BROTH

In saucepan, stir chamomile into broth and heat over medium-high to a gentle boil. Turn heat down to simmer and continue cooking for 2 minutes. Remove from heat and strain through cheesecloth to remove chamomile flowers. Set aside.

PREPARE RISOTTO

Remove langoustine meat from shell and cut in half. Set aside. Heat olive oil and 1 tablespoon butter over medium-high heat until butter melts. Add shallots and sauté until golden. Stir rice into fats for 1½ to 2 minutes.

Stir in white wine to deglaze. When wine has evaporated, begin to add chamomile chicken broth and lobster stock in roughly 2-to-1 proportions, enough to just cover rice. Stir constantly until liquids have evaporated. Repeat addition of liquids to cover rice until it is al dente, about 15 to 20 minutes. Turn heat down to medium and stir in langoustine.

Add more liquid in very small increments to reach desired creaminess, remembering that the butter and mascarpone cheese will make it creamier. Stir in butter pieces, mascarpone cheese, lemon juice, grappa, parsley, salt and pepper.

ASSEMBLE

Divide among 6 plates. Garnish with fresh chamomile flowers, if desired.

**Tip: I like the rice spread out on a plate because, when eating the rice from the edge of the plate to the center, it has better taste, as it's not so hot.*

LEMONY POLENTA-STUFFED CAPPELLACCI WITH RABBIT RAGU AND BLUEBERRY SAUCE

I grew up with polenta in northern Italy, but they never mix polenta with bread or pasta. I broke that rule in my Washington, D.C., restaurants. The filling in the ravioli is polenta. Rabbit and blueberries go into the ragù and marvelously complement each other.

Serves 6
(5 cappellacci per person)

PASTA DOUGH

3 cups, plus 2 tablespoons 00 flour
1 tablespoon semolina flour, plus more for dusting
¼ teaspoon salt
7 egg yolks
1 tablespoon olive oil
1 tablespoon butter, softened, plus more for pan
1 egg
1 tablespoon water
1 tablespoon olive oil
1 tablespoon salt

POLENTA FILLING

2 cups water
3 tablespoons heavy cream
1 tablespoon olive oil
1 teaspoon butter
¼ teaspoon salt
1 cup instant polenta
Zest of 2 lemons
2 tablespoons mascarpone cheese

ROASTED RABBIT

1 (3½-pound) rabbit, bone in, cut in quarters
2 sprigs fresh rosemary, chopped
7 cloves garlic, crushed
½ cup olive oil
Salt, to taste
Freshly ground black pepper, to taste

BLUEBERRIES

1 tablespoon Kirsch liqueur
½ tablespoon sugar
¼ cup water
3 bay leaves
Pinch of freshly ground black pepper
1 cup blueberries

SAUCE

¼ cup olive oil
1 tablespoon butter
3 cloves garlic, chopped
⅓ cup onion, cut into brunoise
⅓ cup carrot, cut into brunoise
⅓ cup celery, cut into brunoise
½ tablespoon rosemary, chopped
⅓ cup white wine
1 cup Rabbit Glacé (page 211)
1 cup Chicken Stock (page 209)
1 tablespoon black olive paste
Salt, to taste
Freshly ground black pepper, to taste

FOR ASSEMBLY

2 tablespoons chives, chopped

PREPARE PASTA

Combine flours and salt in a mixing bowl. Make a well in the center of the flour. Add egg yolks, oil and butter to the well and start to combine, incorporating a little flour at a time, until dough begins to hold together. Work in remaining flour, kneading for about 5 minutes, until dough forms a ball. Cover with a damp towel and let rest for 20 minutes.

PREPARE POLENTA

Combine water, cream, oil, butter and salt in a large saucepan. Bring to a gentle boil. Lower heat to medium. Using a whisk, slowly stir in polenta. Cook for 3 to 5 minutes, stirring constantly, until it forms a wet, doughy consistency. Add lemon zest and mascarpone. Whisk to incorporate. Set aside to cool.

PREPARE RABBIT

Preheat oven to 350°F. Combine all ingredients in a roasting pan and bake for about 30 minutes. Remove from the oven and let cool. Pick meat from bones, dice fine and set aside.

PREPARE BLUEBERRIES

Place Kirsch, sugar, water, bay leaves and pepper in a saucepan and bring to a boil. Cook until it reaches a syrupy consistency. Place pan in ice water and add blueberries. Let cool and set aside.

PREPARE SAUCE

In a medium-size Dutch oven over medium-high heat, place oil and butter and heat until butter is melted and bubbling. Add garlic, onion, carrot, celery and rosemary and sauté until vegetables are soft, about 5 minutes. Deglaze pan with wine. Add reserved rabbit meat and cook for 2 minutes. Add glacé, stock, olive paste, salt and pepper. Simmer for 5 minutes. Set aside.

FINISH PASTA

Cut pasta dough into 8 pieces and cover with plastic wrap. Using a pasta machine and following the manufacturer's directions, roll out each piece of dough to the thickness of a dime. Lay on a cookie sheet lightly dusted with flour. When all the dough has been rolled, refrigerate for 30 minutes.

Place 1 pasta sheet on a lightly floured surface and cut into 3-inch squares. Place a heaping teaspoon of polenta filling in the center of each square. Mix egg and water and use a pastry brush to lightly moisten edges of the square. Fold square in half to form a triangle, pressing down firmly to force out any air and to seal. If necessary, use a toothpick to prick any air pockets. Pinch the air out of the hole, then reseal by pinching the dough together. Bring 2 opposite corners together so the points overlap, then pinch to fasten. Transfer to a cookie sheet lightly dusted with flour. Repeat with remaining dough and filling.

In a large pot, combine water with the oil and salt. Bring to a gentle boil and add the cappellacci. Give them a quick stir so pasta does not stick. Cook for 1½ to 2 minutes. Using a skimmer, transfer cappellacci to a buttered sauté pan.

ASSEMBLE

Gently warm sauce over medium-low heat and divide among 6 plates. Evenly distribute cappellacci over the sauce. Encircle with drops of blueberry sauce. Garnish with chopped chives.

PAPPARDELLE AND LOBSTER WITH HEN OF THE WOODS AND DUCK EGG YOLK

Duck eggs are a delicacy and they taste so much richer than chicken eggs. For a dramatic presentation, the poached egg yolk sits atop the pasta, adding a final flourish of richness to the wide pasta ribbons and chunks of lobster.

Serves 6

SAUCE

20 ounces Pasta Dough (page 210)
3 (1½-pound) lobsters
¼ cup olive oil
¼ cup (1 stick) butter
5 garlic cloves, sliced
1½ pounds hen of the woods (or oyster, chanterelle or shiitake) mushrooms, stemmed and sliced
¼ cup white wine
1 cup Lobster Stock (page 210)
1 cup heavy cream
Salt, to taste
Freshly ground black pepper, to taste
¼ cup parsley, chopped
1 tablespoon black truffle oil

POACHED EGGS

1 quart water
1 teaspoon red wine vinegar
Pinch of salt
6 duck (or chicken) egg yolks

FOR ASSEMBLY

1 tablespoon lobster roe (or tobiko, flying fish roe)
6 sprigs fresh tarragon, 4–5 inches each

PREPARE PASTA

Prepare pasta dough and run it through a pasta machine until the thickness of a dime. Cut into ¾-inch strips. Cover with a cloth and set aside. (You can substitute prepared egg pappardelle.)

PREPARE LOBSTER

To cook lobsters without shell, bring a pot of water to 185°F. For sous vide method, vacuum-pack meat and heat for 5 minutes. Or steam lobsters whole with shell for 12 to 14 minutes. Plunge in ice bath to cool. Remove tail and claw meat. Cut tail meat in half vertically; leave claws whole. Set aside.

PREPARE SAUCE AND FINISH PASTA

Bring 3 quarts salted water to a boil. Cook pasta until al dente and drain. Meanwhile, in a separate sauté pan large enough to hold sauce and pasta, warm oil and butter over medium heat. Sauté garlic until golden. Add mushrooms and cook for 2 to 3 minutes, stirring occasionally. Deglaze pan with wine and cook for 1 to 1½ minutes until liquid is absorbed. Add lobster stock and reduce by one-third. Add lobster, cream, salt and pepper and continue to reduce for 2 to 3 minutes. Add drained pasta to sauce and stir to heat for 2 minutes. Turn off heat and add parsley and truffle oil.

PREPARE POACHED EGGS

Place water, vinegar and salt in a large saucepan and bring to a boil. Remove pan from heat and carefully add egg yolks to cook for 2 minutes. Remove with slotted spoon and place each in a coffee cup, being careful to keep yolks intact.

ASSEMBLE

Divide pasta among 6 plates and place 1 egg atop each serving of pasta. Top with tarragon and roe.

CHOCOLATE RAVIOLI STUFFED WITH ROASTED CARROT AND AMARETTI ON QUAIL RAGÙ

Chocolate with game is the best thing in the world. In Washington, D.C., we made a similar dish. It's a beautiful antidote for a cold winter day. At first, people thought it sounded a little crazy, but once they tried it, they loved it. This dish quickly became our most popular.

Serves 6
(5 ravioli per person)

PASTA FILLING

2 pounds carrots
3 sprigs fresh rosemary
⅓ cup olive oil
¼ teaspoon salt
1 tablespoon mostarda di Cremona
¼ cup amaretti cookies

PASTA DOUGH

3 cups, plus 2 tablespoons 00 flour
1 tablespoon semolina flour, plus more for dusting
¼ teaspoon salt
½ cup cocoa powder
7 egg yolks
½ tablespoon olive oil
1 tablespoon butter, softened
1 egg
1 tablespoon water

VEAL GLACÉ

1 gallon Veal Stock (page 213)
3 liters Malbec wine (or other red wine)
6 cloves garlic, smashed
4 sprigs fresh rosemary
1 cup sugar

RAGÙ

⅓ cup extra-virgin olive oil
1 tablespoon butter
1 tablespoon sprigs fresh rosemary, chopped
⅓ cup onion, finely diced
⅓ cup carrots, finely diced
⅓ cup celery, finely diced
1 teaspoon garlic, finely diced
3 bay leaves
10 quail, deboned and chopped
¼ cup white wine
1 cup Veal Glacé (see above)
1 cup Chicken Stock (page 209)
Sea salt, to taste
Freshly ground black pepper, to taste

FOR ASSEMBLY

1 tablespoon extra-virgin olive oil
1 tablespoon salt
2 tablespoons butter
Dark chocolate, shaved
Chives, chopped

PREPARE PASTA FILLING

Preheat oven to 400°F. Toss carrots with rosemary and oil. Roast in oven for 1 hour or until tender. Purée in a food processor until smooth. Place cheesecloth inside a fine-mesh sieve and place over a bowl. Place the carrot purée in the cheesecloth and strain in the refrigerator for 8 to 12 hours to extract liquid. Return to food processor and pulse with salt, mostarda di Cremona and cookies. If filling is not dry, you'll need to add more cookies.

PREPARE PASTA DOUGH

Combine flours, salt and cocoa powder in a mixing bowl. Make a well in the center of the flour. Add egg yolks, oil and butter to the well and start to combine, incorporating a little flour at a time, until dough begins to hold together. Work in remaining flour, kneading for about 5 minutes, until dough forms a ball. Cover with a damp towel and let rest for 20 minutes.

PREPARE VEAL GLACÉ

In a wide, shallow pan, add wine, sugar, garlic and rosemary. Bring to low boil and reduce to a simmer, and reduce until the consistency coats the back of a spoon. Add wine reduction to the reduced stock and strain through a fine-mesh chinois and reserve.

PREPARE RAGÙ

In a medium Dutch oven over medium-high heat, place oil and butter, and heat until butter is melted and bubbling. Add rosemary, onion, carrot, celery, garlic and bay leaves and sauté until vegetables are soft, about 5 minutes. Add quail and cook for 2 to 3 minutes. Deglaze pan with wine and cook for 3 minutes. Add glacé, stock, salt and pepper. Simmer for 8 minutes and set aside.

FINISH PASTA

Cut dough into 8 pieces and cover with plastic wrap. Using a pasta machine and following the manufacturer's directions, roll out each piece of dough to the thickness of a dime. Lay on a cookie sheet lightly dusted with flour. When all the dough has been rolled, refrigerate for 30 minutes. Lay out 1 sheet of pasta dough horizontally on a clean working surface dusted with flour. Mix egg and water and moisten pasta using a pastry brush. On the half of the sheet closest to you, evenly space 1-tablespoon portions of the filling, about a finger's width apart. Fold top half of pasta sheet over filling. Seal edges by pressing fingers between filling and along the bottom. Cut into equal-size squares. Pinch edges of ravioli to check that no air is trapped inside. If necessary, use a toothpick to prick any air pockets. Pinch air out of the hole, then reseal by pinching dough back together. Place ravioli on a cookie sheet lightly dusted with flour. Repeat with remaining dough and filling.

ASSEMBLE

Place just enough water to cook pasta in a large pot. Add oil and salt and bring to a gentle boil. Add ravioli. Give them a quick stir to make sure they do not stick to the bottom. Cook for 1½ to 2 minutes. Using a skimmer, transfer ravioli to a sauté pan with butter.

Gently warm ragù over medium heat and divide sauce among 6 plates. Evenly distribute ravioli over sauce on each plate. Garnish with chives and chocolate.

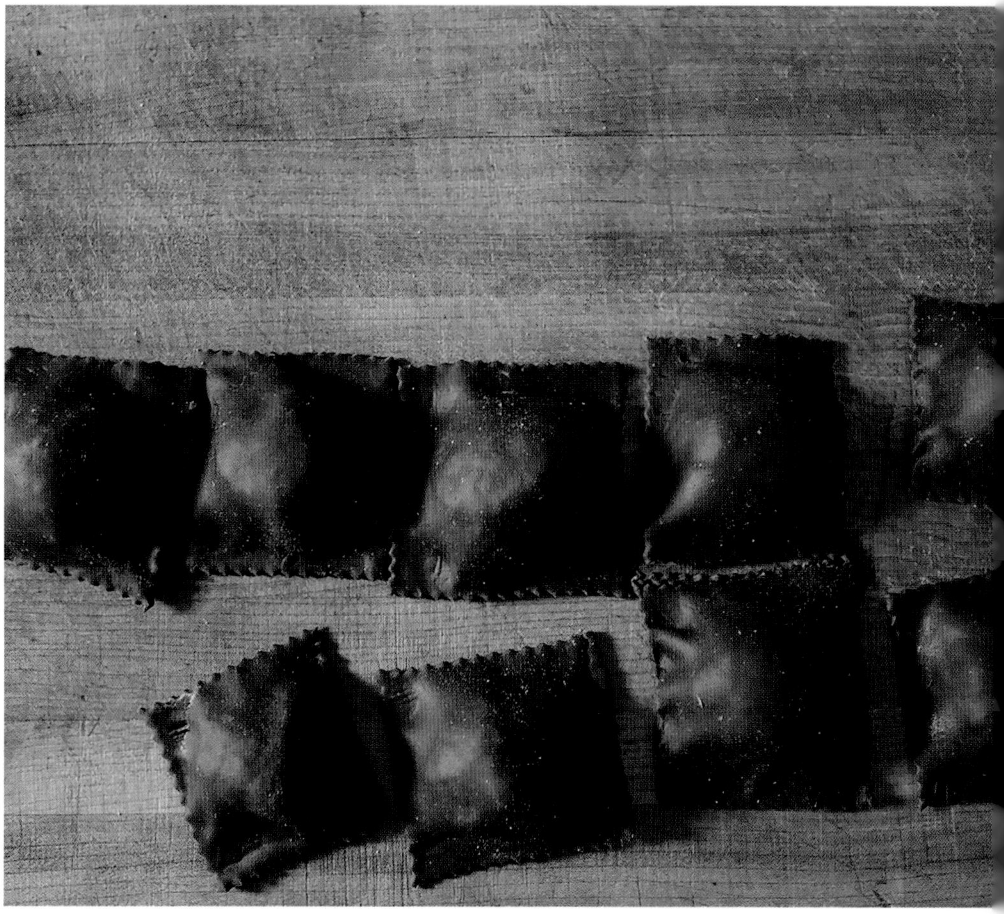

LOBSTER RISOTTO WITH ROASTED TOMATO AND WHITE TRUFFLE PERFUME

You shouldn't be intimidated at the prospect of making risotto. It just requires attention and lots of stirring. It's one of those things you get better at with practice—to know just the perfect point of doneness for the rice. The roasted tomatoes, lobster and truffle perfume give this one so much flavor.

Serves 6

ROASTED TOMATOES

2 medium-size plum tomatoes, halved lengthwise
Pinch of salt
Pinch of dried oregano
Extra-virgin olive oil

GARLIC-INFUSED OLIVE OIL

3 garlic cloves, halved lengthwise
½ cup extra-virgin olive oil
Sea salt, to taste
Freshly ground black pepper, to taste

RISOTTO

¾ pound lobster meat, cooked
1 tablespoon Garlic-Infused Olive Oil (see above)
½ white onion, chopped
1½ cups Acquerello Carnaroli rice
½ cup dry white wine
4–5 cups Lobster Stock (page 210) (or seafood or vegetable stock)
½ cup Tomato Sauce (page 212)
10 leaves fresh basil, finely chopped
⅓ cup, plus 2 teaspoons unsalted butter
1 tablespoon Italian parsley, chopped, plus extra for garnish
2 tablespoons white truffle oil
Sea salt, to taste
Freshly ground black pepper, to taste
Grated Parmesan cheese (optional)

PREPARE ROASTED TOMATOES (6 hours ahead)

Season tomato halves with salt and oregano. Place in a colander. Let tomatoes sit for 2 hours to remove moisture and concentrate flavors.

Preheat oven to 125°F.

Line a baking sheet with aluminum foil. Place tomatoes, cut side down, on foil. Drizzle with olive oil and roast for 3 to 4 hours, until tomatoes are slightly shrunken and cooked but not dry.

Remove from oven and cool for about 5 minutes before handling. Remove skins if desired.

MAKE GARLIC OLIVE OIL (1 hour ahead)

Place garlic and olive oil in a small saucepan over lowest heat possible. Heat for 1 hour or until garlic becomes very soft and infuses oil. Remove garlic. Season to taste.

PREPARE RISOTTO

Cut lobster meat into ½-inch cubes.

In a heavy-bottomed pot over medium-high heat, place garlic oil. Add onion and sauté, stirring constantly, taking care not to brown.

Add rice and cook, stirring, for about 2 minutes. Add wine and stir constantly until absorbed.

Add stock, about ½ cup at a time, stirring constantly and adding more as liquid is absorbed. Continue process until rice is soft and creamy, but slightly al dente. *(Note: some brands of rice may require extra stock to reach desired doneness.)*

Add roasted tomatoes, tomato sauce, basil and lobster meat, continuing to stir. Cook mixture for another 4 minutes. Stir in butter, parsley, truffle oil, salt and pepper. Stir well to combine all ingredients. Serve warm. Garnish with parsley and grated Parmesan, if using.

INSIDE OUT TORTELLI WITH BURRATA, HONEY, MINT AND SHRIMP

I thought this would be an amusing way to keep the spirit of the traditional tortelli dish—by serving the stuffing on the outside, sort of a deconstructed version. The soft, fresh Burrata melts in your mouth—a wonderful complement to the shrimp.

Serves 6

TORTELLI

1½ pounds Pasta Dough (page 210)
3 tablespoons butter
1 tablespoon fresh thyme leaves

SHRIMP STOCK

10 pounds shrimp, head on
15 pounds ice cubes
½ cup grapeseed oil
2 cups onion, sliced
1 cup carrots, roughly cut
1 cup celery, diced
1 cup leeks, diced
1 cup fennel, diced
4 cloves garlic
½ cup cream sherry
2 cups white wine
5 sprigs fresh thyme
5 sprigs fresh tarragon
5 sprigs lemon verbena
20 white peppercorns

SHRIMP RAGÙ

¼ cup celery, diced
¼ cup onion, diced
¼ cup carrot, diced
1 teaspoon garlic, minced
2 tablespoons extra-virgin olive oil
1 pound shrimp, deshelled, deveined and cut into small pieces
2 tablespoons thyme leaves
⅓ cup white wine
½ cup Chicken Stock (page 209)
½ cup Shrimp Stock (see above)
⅛ teaspoon salt
⅛ teaspoon freshly ground black pepper
¼ cup butter

FOR ASSEMBLY

8 ounces fresh Burrata, chopped
1 tablespoon honey
⅛ cup mint, finely chopped

PREPARE TORTELLI

Roll out portions of pasta dough through a pasta machine on the #3 setting. Cut pasta sheet into 2 x 2–inch squares using a pastry cutter. Fold square in half diagonally to make a triangle. Place thumb over folded side. Fold 2 opposite corners over thumb so points overlap. Fold the third point backward. Repeat process for remaining squares and pasta sheets.

PREPARE SHRIMP STOCK

Heat oil in a 20-quart stockpot over high heat. Sauté the shrimp until they are evenly browned, 6 to 8 minutes. Add onions, carrots, celery, leeks, fennel and garlic and sauté for 5 to 7 minutes, until they are tender. Add the cream sherry and reduce to 2 tablespoons. Add the white wine and reduce to ½ cup. Add the ice, thyme, tarragon, lemon verbena and peppercorns and bring to a simmer over medium heat. Skim off any impurities or fats that rise to the top. Simmer for 30 minutes and strain through a fine-mesh chinois. Reduce to 1 gallon, strain again, and chill over the ice.

PREPARE SHRIMP RAGÙ

Sauté celery, onion, carrots, garlic and olive oil in a large sauté pan over medium-high heat for 1 minute. Add shrimp and thyme and cook for 1 minute more, stirring constantly. Deglaze with wine. Add stocks, salt and pepper. Cook for 2 to 3 minutes. Remove from heat and add butter.

FINISH TORTELLI

Cook tortelli in salted boiling water for 1 to 2 minutes. Drain and place in a large sauté pan with butter and thyme. Lightly sauté over medium-high heat.

ASSEMBLE

Divide shrimp ragù among 6 plates. Place tortelli over sauce. Top each tortelli with small pieces of Burrata and drizzle with honey and mint.

BIGOLI AND OCTOPUS WITH AMATRICIANA SAUCE

It's very Venetian to serve bigoli pasta with duck or anchovies. I was drinking wine and talking Italian food with my wife, Ingrid, and a friend one day. Ingrid had the idea that Amatriciana sauce would be good with bigoli, and my friend loves octopus. So there it was. This dish was born of food we remember and love.

Serves 6

BIGOLI PASTA DOUGH

3 cups whole wheat flour
1 cup all-purpose flour
4 egg yolks
Salt, to taste
½ cup milk
2 tablespoons butter
1 cup semolina flour, for dusting

OCTOPUS

1 gallon water
Salt, to taste
1 lemon, halved
3 bay leaves
½ cup white wine
1 tablespoon white wine vinegar
½ tablespoon black peppercorns
2 pounds octopus
3 wine corks

AMATRICIANA SAUCE

1 cup smoked pancetta, chopped
¾ cup extra-virgin olive oil
5 cloves garlic, sliced
1 white onion, chopped
1 tablespoon fresh rosemary, chopped
1 tablespoon sage, chopped
1½ pounds cooked octopus, cut into 1-inch pieces
1 cup white wine
3 cups Roasted Tomatoes (page 99)
1 cup Chicken Stock (page 209)
½ teaspoon red pepper flakes
Salt, to taste
Freshly ground black pepper, to taste

FOR ASSEMBLY

⅓ cup Italian parsley
½ cup pecorino cheese, grated

PREPARE BIGOLI

Place flours in the bowl of a standing mixer. In a large bowl, place egg yolks and salt. Heat milk and butter until lukewarm and add to yolk mixture. Combine with flours until a smooth dough forms. It should be soft but not sticky. Remove rotary blade from a meat grinder and pass dough through a ¼-inch die, or use a pasta machine fitted with the thick spaghetti die. Cut long strings of pasta to the length of spaghetti. Place on a cookie sheet and dust with semolina flour. Set aside.

PREPARE OCTOPUS

Bring water to a boil in a large stockpot with salt, lemon, bay leaves, wine, vinegar and peppercorns. When boiling, add octopus and wine corks and simmer for 40 to 45 minutes. Remove octopus from liquid and slice into bite-size pieces.

PREPARE AMATRICIANA SAUCE

Cook pancetta in ½ cup olive oil in a large saucepan over medium-high heat for 1 minute. Add garlic, onion, rosemary and sage and cook for 5 minutes. Add octopus and cook for 1 minute. Add wine and cook for 1 minute. Add roasted tomato and cook for 3 minutes, then add stock and red pepper flakes and simmer for 3 to 4 minutes. Season to taste and reserve sauce in pan.

ASSEMBLE

Bring 1 gallon salted water to a boil in a large stockpot and add pasta. Boil for 3 minutes. Drain pasta and add to pan sauce. Add remaining olive oil and the parsley. Toss in the pan for 1 to 2 minutes, then divide evenly among 6 plates. Finish each plate with grated cheese.

MEZZELUNE AND STRACCHINO WITH VENUS CLAMS, SOPPRESSATA AND FAVA BEANS

Stracchino is a wonderfully soft cow cheese that's just a little sour yet delicate, almost sweet and sour, but more on the sour side. It was one of those things the working-class people would eat; our mothers fed it to us for something light to eat if we weren't feeling well.

So I've given it a big promotion here, pairing it with clams—a great match. It's something I often prepare for my Chef's Table, but everything must be made fresh just at mealtime—yes, even the pasta!

Serves 6

MEZZELUNE

1½ pounds Pasta Dough (page 210)
2 eggs, beaten
1 pound fresh stracchino cheese, divided into ¼-ounce balls

CLAMS

4½ ounces Venus clams
4 cloves garlic, smashed
2 tablespoons extra-virgin olive oil
1 cup white wine
2 sprigs fresh thyme

CLAM SAUCE

½ cup soppressata, julienned
2 teaspoons thyme leaves
2 tablespoons extra-virgin olive oil
¼ cup white wine
¾ cup Raisin Tomatoes (page 35)
¾ cup fava beans, boiled and peeled
3 tablespoons butter
⅛ cup Italian parsley, chopped
Salt, to taste
Freshly ground black pepper, to taste

PREPARE MEZZELUNE

Roll out pasta dough through a pasta machine on the #2 setting. Cut with a 2½-inch-round ravioli cutter. Brush edges of the pasta with a pastry brush dipped into beaten eggs. Place stracchino cheese balls in the middle of each pasta circle and fold over to make half-moon shapes. Press edges to seal. Repeat process for remaining dough and cheese.

PREPARE CLAMS

Sauté clams with garlic, olive oil, white wine and thyme until clams open up. Remove clams from shells and reserve 1 cup of their cooking liquid.

PREPARE CLAM SAUCE

Sauté soppressata, thyme and oil in a large sauté pan over medium-high heat for 2 minutes. Deglaze with wine. Add reserved clam stock, the tomatoes, fava beans and clam meat. Simmer to reduce liquid by half. Remove from heat and add butter and parsley. Season to taste and reserve sauce in pan.

PREPARE PASTA

Cook pasta in salted boiling water for 1½ to 2 minutes. Drain and transfer to pan with sauce. Cook for 1 to 2 minutes while tossing. Divide sauced pasta equally among 6 plates.

BLACK INK CUTTLEFISH RISOTTO WITH BAKED SHEEP RICOTTA AND FAVA BEANS

Cuttlefish is a Venetian favorite and always brings back good memories from childhood fishing trips. Similar to calamari, but meatier, the salty sea flavor of the cuttlefish contrasts nicely with the earthiness of the fava beans and ricotta cheese.

Serves 6

CUTTLEFISH

½ cup celery, diced
½ cup onion, diced
½ cup olive oil
5 garlic cloves, minced
2 sprigs rosemary, finely chopped
2 pounds cuttlefish, cleaned and cut into 2-inch pieces
1 cup red wine
2 tablespoons red wine vinegar
4 cups Vegetable Stock (page 213)
3 bay leaves
1 cup Tomato Sauce (page 212)
½ cup tomato paste
3 cuttlefish ink sacs (or 1 teaspoon black squid ink)
Salt, to taste
Freshly ground black pepper, to taste

FOR ASSEMBLY

½ cup fava beans
½ cup dried ricotta cheese, grated

RISOTTO

4 garlic cloves, minced
½ cup olive oil
2 cups Acquerello Carnaroli rice
½ cup white wine
8 cups Vegetable Stock (page 213)
½ cup butter
½ cup Italian parsley, chopped
Salt, to taste
Freshly ground black pepper, to taste

PREPARE CUTTLEFISH

Place celery, onion, oil and garlic in a food processor and blend until smooth. Add rosemary, then place in a large saucepan over medium-high heat. Cook for 3 minutes. Add cuttlefish and cook for 6 to 8 minutes. Add red wine, vinegar, stock, bay leaves, tomato sauce and tomato paste. Break open the ink sacs and strain through a fine-mesh sieve as you add ink to the sauce, watching closely to prevent sand from getting into the sauce. The cuttlefish will become a deep black color. Reduce heat to medium and continue to cook for 35 to 40 minutes, until tender. Remove from heat and let cool.

PREPARE FAVA BEANS

Shell fava beans and blanch in salted boiling water for 1 to 2 minutes. Drain and place in ice water. Drain and remove second shells from beans. Reserve for plating.

PREPARE RISOTTO

Place garlic and ¼ cup olive oil in a large heavy-bottomed Dutch oven. Sauté for 2 minutes over medium-high heat. Add rice and cook, stirring, for about 2 minutes. Add wine and stir constantly until wine is absorbed. Add stock in ½-cup increments, stirring constantly, until broth has been absorbed and rice is al dente. Add cuttlefish, continuing to stir, and cook for 4 minutes. Add butter, parsley and remaining oil, then season to taste. Stir until everything is well combined.

**Note: Add more vegetable stock as needed; amount varies with the brand of rice and how quickly the stock evaporates.*

ASSEMBLE

Divide risotto evenly among 6 bowls and top with fava beans and dried ricotta.

SAFFRON TAGLIERINI CARBONARA WITH SEA URCHIN AND GUANCIALE

Sea urchin is one of my favorite things to eat. It tastes like honey from the sea. Raw, with its sweet and salty notes, it's the crowning touch to the silky narrow taglierini sautéed with guanicale. This is the most exciting carbonara ever.

Serves 6

PASTA

Basic Pasta Dough (page 210)
½ teaspoon saffron
1 tablespoon olive oil
1 teaspoon salt

SAUCE

2 cups heavy cream
1 tablespoon mascarpone
½ cup Parmesan, grated
5 egg yolks
2 tablespoons fresh parsley, chopped
Sea salt, to taste
1 teaspoon coarsely ground black pepper
1 tablespoon butter
½ cup guanciale (or pancetta), diced
1 cup Lobster Stock (page 210)
18 to 30 pieces raw sea urchin, enough for 3 to 5 pieces per person

PREPARE PASTA

In a large pot, bring water, salt and olive oil to a boil. Add pasta and cook at a medium boil until al dente, 2 to 3 minutes, depending on pasta's freshness. Dry pasta takes a little longer to cook. Drain.

PREPARE SAUCE

In a stand-up mixer bowl, mix together cream, mascarpone, Parmesan, egg yolks, parsley, salt and pepper. Set aside. Melt butter in a large sauté pan. Add guanciale and sauté until slightly crisp. Add stock and reduce by half. Toss in cooked pasta and stir to coat. Reduce heat. Stir in cream and egg mixture. Simmer without boiling for about 2 minutes, until sauce is slightly thickened enough to coat spoon.

ASSEMBLE

Divide pasta among plates and garnish with sea urchin on top. Enjoy.

EVOLUTION of a TOMATO

I like to use the tomato as an analogy for the beauty of pure food and the use of quality ingredients.

I am talking about real tomatoes here, not the fake, made-for-supermarkets versions. The best tomato you can eat is the ugliest tomato you can find. Even though it's so ugly, it's also naturally beautiful. It's not the tomato that looks like every other tomato on the shelf, or the one that looks too perfect to be true.

Beauty is more than skin deep. In Italy, we have a saying "Is not gold, everything shiny." We are so brainwashed about our produce these days that we think it should be perfect looking. But when you slice that perfect-looking tomato, it has no flavor. Your eyes have deceived you. Mother Nature is not about perfection. Never buy a wrapped tomato. Never buy tomatoes that have been refrigerated.

Don't let your eyes make all your decisions. I can tell by touch and smell if it is a truly beautiful tomato—one brimming with flavor. You bite into this tomato and you think, "This has such great flavor, I wonder how it would taste with a little garlic, or a little mozzarella, or a little basil?" And that's how the tomato evolution began. To evolve, one must first create.

The tomato is so important to Italian cuisine, yet ironically it comes from the New World, not the Old World. Tomato sauce, caprese salad, tomato juice . . . the evolution continues. And we continue to evolve it further. Tomato marmalade. Tomato caviar. Tomato confit. Raisin tomatoes. Crazy bubbling tomato! All are wonderful evolutions we have developed around the singular flavor of one central, elemental ingredient.

FISH

A GREAT CATCH

Fresh and Simple

‡

Growing up in Venice, we would go out fishing and catch all of our own seafood. We ate a lot of flounder, sardines, branzino, cuttlefish, calamari, stone crab, smelt, mussels and clams. This was considered "poor-people food" back then—funny how time changes things. Nowadays, this would qualify as food for the nobility.

The most important thing to remember when preparing seafood is to keep it as simple as possible. If it's not fresh, don't try to disguise it—just don't use it. Fresh fish doesn't need a lot of heavy sauces or strong seasonings. When you smother the naturally delicate flavor of the fish, you are committing culinary sin.

My recipes, at first glance, may appear complicated. But really they are all about simplicity. Simplicity is my mantra. I believe all food, especially seafood, tastes best in its most basic state. My recipes incorporate vegetables, fruit and other side dishes to complement the fish. They require a little preparation because the fish deserves worthy accompaniments. After all, you wouldn't put on a necktie and suit jacket with shorts and sneakers, would you? So take the time to give your guests something beautiful on the plate.

Finally, don't let anyone tell you that you cannot drink red wine with fish. I love a nice, light red with seafood. Always follow and trust your own palate!

HALIBUT WITH RHUBARB-STRAWBERRY SAUCE

While this might seem an unlikely combination, the rhubarb and strawberry bring a sweetness and acidity to the delicate halibut that let you know the three were meant for each other.

Serves 6

RHUBARB-STRAWBERRY SAUCE

4½ tablespoons cold butter, divided
1½ cups rhubarb, diced, strings removed
1 cup strawberries, stemmed and chopped
¼ cup sugar
2 tablespoons champagne vinegar
2 tablespoons white balsamic vinegar
1 cup Strawberry Juice (208)
1 tablespoon lemon juice
1 tablespoon orange juice
½ cup Prosecco
1 tablespoon red beet juice
Sea salt, to taste

HALIBUT

18 baby rainbow carrots, stems removed
6 (6-ounce) halibut fillets
Sea salt, to taste
Freshly ground pepper, to taste
¼ cup grapeseed oil
2 tablespoons butter, divided
½ teaspoon lavender leaves

FOR ASSEMBLY

6 strawberries, stemmed and quartered
1 teaspoon rosemary flowers

PREPARE SAUCE

Melt ½ tablespoon of butter in a saucepan over medium heat. Add rhubarb, strawberries and sugar. Cook for 3 to 4 minutes until sugar is fully dissolved. Add vinegars and let cook for 1½ to 2 minutes. Add strawberry juice, lemon juice, orange juice, Prosecco and red beet juice. Cook for another 2 minutes until the mixture reaches the consistency of a light syrup. Remove a few pieces of rhubarb for garnish and mix the rest together in a blender until silky smooth. Pass through a chinois or other sieve. Return sauce to the saucepan and whisk in the remaining butter, a little at a time. Add a small amount of water if too thick.

PREPARE HALIBUT

Preheat oven to 375°F. Boil or steam carrots until tender; drain in colander and set aside. Season both sides of halibut. In a large sauté pan, heat grapeseed oil and 1 tablespoon butter over high heat. Pan-sear fish skin-side up for 1 minute, then flip and cook for 1 more minute. Place pan in the oven for 5 to 6 minutes, depending on thickness of fish, until fish turns opaque. Add lavender and 1 tablespoon butter. Cook 1 more minute over medium heat, basting fish with butter in the pan.

ASSEMBLE

Divide fish among 6 plates and spoon sauce around one side. Toss carrots in pan juices and arrange on other side of fish. Garnish with fresh chopped strawberries, reserved diced rhubarb and rosemary flowers.

ÔRA KING SALMON WITH BELUGA LENTILS, BABY TURNIPS AND MUSTARD SAUCE

We use Ôra king salmon from New Zealand, raised in one of the world's most sustainable farms, but you can substitute any high-quality salmon. When you enjoy this dish, try the pear first to let its sweetness cleanse the palate. Then sample each component individually before mixing and matching the variety of flavors.

Serves 6

BELUGA LENTILS

⅓ cup olive oil
⅓ cup (1 medium) carrots, sliced
⅓ cup (1 stalk) celery, chopped
⅓ cup (⅓ medium) Vidalia onion, chopped
1 teaspoon fresh thyme leaves
2 ounces prosciutto, whole slices
1 quart Chicken Stock (page 209)
2 cups beluga lentils
Sea salt, to taste
Freshly ground black pepper, to taste

BABY TURNIPS

6 baby turnips
1 cup water, room temperature
2 tablespoons honey
2 tablespoons light brown sugar, loosely packed
2 tablespoons champagne vinegar
1 black peppercorn
1 teaspoon butter

MUSTARD SAUCE

½ cup Chicken Stock (page 209)
2 cups heavy cream
2 teaspoons Dijon mustard
⅛ teaspoon cumin
⅛ teaspoon turmeric
⅛ teaspoon tarragon

SALMON

6 (7-ounce) fillets or steaks Ôra king (or other) salmon
Sea salt, to taste
Freshly ground black pepper, to taste
¼ cup grapeseed or canola oil
¼ cup butter
6 Roasted Pear halves (page 212)

PREPARE LENTILS

Heat olive oil in a small pot over medium heat. Add carrots, celery, onion, thyme and prosciutto. Sauté for 2 minutes. Add stock, lentils, salt and pepper. Bring to a boil, then simmer until lentils are al dente, 25 to 28 minutes. Drain and remove prosciutto.

PREPARE TURNIPS

Trim turnip greens, leaving ½ to 1 inch. If preparing by sous vide method, combine water, honey, brown sugar, vinegar, peppercorn and butter with turnips in sous vide bag and cook at 145°F for 20-22 minutes until tender but firm. Otherwise, place water, honey, brown sugar, vinegar, peppercorn and butter in a medium pot. Bring to a simmer and add turnips. Cover and cook for 5 to 7 minutes, until turnips are tender but firm. When cooked, add ice to liquid to preserve the green stem color.

PREPARE SAUCE

Put chicken stock in a large saucepan over medium heat. Reduce by one-third. Add cream, mustard, cumin, turmeric and tarragon. Bring to a boil over medium-high heat, stirring occasionally. Lower heat to medium and continue to boil 4 to 5 minutes, stirring occasionally, until thick enough to coat the back of a spoon.

PREPARE SALMON

Preheat oven to 375°F. Season both sides of the fish to taste. Heat oil over high heat in a large ovenproof sauté pan. Pan-sear salmon, skin side up, quickly for 1 minute, then flip to sear for 1 minute on other side. Place pan with salmon in the oven for 5 to 6 minutes, depending on thickness, until medium rare (red in center) or longer if desired. Remove from oven and place butter on top of fish. Cook 1 minute over medium heat, basting fish with butter.

ASSEMBLE

Spread lentils over a platter and top with salmon. Drizzle sauce over salmon. Cut pear halves into ¼-inch-thick slices, leaving intact at small end, and fan slices around fish. Arrange turnips to side of fish.

TURBOT WITH LOBSTER MILK SHAKE, GOLD BEETS AND WARM GREEN-PEA MAYONNAISE

A lobster milk shake? Don't be put off—it's really more like a rich, savory sauce that's served in a shot glass and poured over the turbot just before you dig into this luscious and colorful dish.

Serves 6

WARM MAYONNAISE

4 tablespoon Mayonnaise (page 210)
½ tablespoon lemon juice
2 tablespoon Green Pea Purée (page 211)

BEETS

12 baby gold beets
2 tablespoons honey
½ cup water

LOBSTER MILK SHAKE

1 tablespoon grapeseed oil
2 cloves garlic, crushed
1 (½-pound) whole lobster, butterflied
¼ cup fennel, chopped
2 tablespoons fresh ginger, minced
½ tablespoon saffron
½ tablespoon turmeric
1 (5-inch) sprig thyme
Pinch Spanish paprika
Pinch cayenne
½ tablespoon Pernod
2 tablespoons cognac
½ cup tomato juice
2 quarts Lobster Stock (page 210)
½ cup Crème Fraîche (209)
1 tablespoon fresh lime juice
Sea salt, to taste
Freshly ground pepper, to taste
1 tablespoon butter, cold

TURBOT

3½ cups extra-virgin olive oil
3½ cups butter
3 (5-inch) sprigs thyme
10 lavender leaves
Sea salt, to taste
6 (6-ounce) turbot fillets
Freshly ground pepper, to taste

GARNISH

30 candy or grape tomatoes
2 tablespoons Tomato Marmalade (page 212)

MAKE MAYONNAISE

Combine mayonnaise, lemon and pea puree. Before serving, bring water to boil in a saucepan and heat the mayonnaise in a bowl set into the water, stirring, for 1 minute.

PREPARE BEETS

Wash beets thoroughly and cut off greens, leaving 1-inch stems. Sous vide with honey and water 25 minutes at 175°F. Alternately, wrap beets in foil and roast for 25 minutes at 400°F or boil with honey in enough water to cover for 25 minutes. Chill in ice bath and peel using a towel. Cut beets in half to serve.

PREPARE MILK SHAKE

Heat grapeseed oil in a small stockpot over medium-high heat. Add garlic and whole lobster with cut side down. Cook for 2½ to 3 minutes. Flip lobster and add fennel, ginger, saffron, turmeric, thyme, paprika, cayenne, Pernod and cognac. Cook 1 more minute until lobster meat turns solid white. Remove lobster and add tomato juice and lobster stock.

Simmer for 35 minutes to reduce by one-third Add crème fraîche and continue to cook for 20 minutes. Remove pan from heat and strain the solids. Remove meat from tail and claws and put in a blender with strained broth, lime juice, salt and pepper. Add butter and blend until frothy.

PREPARE TURBOT

Heat olive oil, butter, 3 sprigs thyme and lavender over low heat, about 120°F. Add fish until cooked through. Remove with a spatula and pat dry with paper towels to remove oil. Season to taste.

ASSEMBLE

Divide the fish among 6 plates. Add a dollop of warmed mayonnaise and beets to the side. Pour lobster shake into 6 shot glasses and serve to the side. Garnish plate with dots of tomato marmalade and candy tomatoes. At the table, pour lobster shake over the fish.

VANILLA SALT-CRUSTED BRANZINO WITH BLOOD ORANGE SAUCE AND CAMPARI CIPOLLINI

I love blood oranges with fish. One day, sitting at the Sea Salt bar, I tried a slice of orange spritzed with Campari, and I knew I was on to something with the bitter playing off the sweet. Salt-crusted fish is not uncommon, but here the addition of vanilla really brings the whole dish together.

Serves 6

CAMPARI CIPOLLINI

18 cipollini onions, peeled
6 tablespoons Campari
¼ cup sugar
¼ cup orange juice
¾ cup Prosecco
1 teaspoon salt
½ cup water
¼ cup white balsamic vinegar

BRANZINO

3 (1¾-pound) whole branzinos, scaled and gutted
3 sprigs fresh thyme
1 blood orange, wedged into 9 pieces
White pepper, to taste

SALT CRUST

7 egg whites
5 pounds rock salt
1 tablespoon vanilla extract

BLOOD ORANGE SAUCE

2 cups blood orange juice
½ teaspoon saffron
Pinch cayenne pepper
½ cup Prosecco
3 sprigs fresh thyme, stemmed
1 tablespoon lemon juice
½ teaspoon salt
1 tablespoons sugar
4 tablespoons cold butter, cubed
1 tablespoon chives, chopped

PREPARE CIPOLLINI

Combine all ingredients in a small saucepot. Bring to a boil over medium-high heat. Reduce heat and let simmer for 25 to 30 minutes. Remove onions with a slotted spoon. Reduce liquid to a light, syrup-like consistency. Return cipollini to liquid. Set aside.

PREPARE BRANZINO

Stuff each stomach cavity of branzino with thyme and 3 orange wedges. Season exterior of each branzino with white pepper.

PREPARE SALT CRUST

In the bowl of a standing mixer, whisk egg whites until soft peaks form. Combine with rock salt and vanilla until mixed well. On a cookie sheet lined with parchment paper, make 3 small, ¼-inch-thick beds of salt in the shape of a fish. Place each prepared fish on a bed of salt. Cover each fish with remaining salt, being sure to enclose the entire fish.

PREPARE FISH

Preheat oven to 350°F. Bake fish for 25 minutes.

PREPARE BLOOD ORANGE SAUCE

Combine juice, saffron, cayenne, Prosecco, thyme, lemon juice, salt and sugar in a saucepan. Bring to a gentle boil and reduce by one-third. Remove from heat and slowly whisk in butter, 1 piece at a time, until butter has melted.

FILLET FISH

Crack salt crust into pieces as large as possible and remove, exposing top of fish. Remove meat from bones with a spatula, being careful to leave the backbone in place. Remove spine of fish and discard. Separate bottom fillet from its skin. Watch for bones; there will be a heavy concentration of bones in the belly area of the fish.

ASSEMBLE

Divide cipollini onions among 6 dishes. Place 1 branzino fillet on each plate and spoon sauce over fish. Finish with chives.

JOHN DORY WITH GARDEN PEAS AND PROSECCO NAGE

John Dory is a pretty popular fish in Italy. They call it "St. Peter" there because, according to one legend, when the saintly fisherman grabbed a John Dory, two black marks appeared, one on each side of its body. The devout believed these were the fingerprints of St. Peter. No matter where the name originated, this is a dish you want to eat on a warm summer day.

Serves 6

VEGETABLES

18 green pea pods
18 baby red onions, trimmed
18 green beans
1 cup green peas, shelled
18 snow peas, strings removed
30 fava beans, shelled
3 tablespoons red bell pepper, diced

NAGE

2 cups Fish Fumet (page 209)
½ cup Prosecco
½ teaspoon saffron
Pinch cayenne pepper
3 (5-inch) sprigs fresh thyme, leaves removed
½ teaspoon sea salt
1 tablespoon lemon juice
4 tablespoons cold butter, cut into small pieces

FISH

3 cup Fish Fumet (page 209)
1½ cups water, room temperature
½ cup dry white wine
1 lemon, sliced
5 bay leaves
10 black peppercorns
6 (6-ounce) John Dory fillets
Sea salt, to taste
Freshly ground black pepper, to taste

MAKE VEGETABLES

Bring 6 cups water to a boil in a medium pot over high heat. While it's heating, prepare an ice bath by adding cold water to ice cubes. With a sharp knife, cut a thin slice off the string side of each pea pod to expose peas. Place in the boiling water along with baby red onions and green beans. After ½ minute, add shelled green peas, snow peas and fava beans. Continue to cook for 1 minute. Drain and chill vegetables in ice bath. Remove and pat dry with paper towels. Peel skins from shelled fava beans and, including diced bell peppers, add to vegetables.

PREPARE NAGE

In large saucepan over medium heat, combine 2 cups fish fumet, Prosecco, saffron, cayenne, thyme, salt and lemon juice. Cook down for 3 minutes. Stir in butter, one piece at a time, until all is used. Cook until nage reaches a light syrupy consistency.

MAKE FISH

In a large sauté pan over low heat, combine 3 cups fish fumet, water, wine, lemon slices, bay leaves and peppercorns. Bring to simmer. Add fish and poach gently for 5 minutes, flipping the fish halfway through the cooking process. When fish has turned solid white, remove pan from burner. Season to taste.

ASSEMBLE

Divide the vegetables among 6 plates and top with nage and fish.

PAN-SEARED BLACK GROUPER WITH BLACK TRUFFLE BUTTER, FAVA BEANS AND SMOKED-SALT FINGERLING POTATOES

Four words: Summer on a plate. The Italian black truffle season runs from May until September, which is also when fava beans are at their peak. We keep serving this elegant dish at Sea Salt as long into fall as we can keep getting fresh ingredients.

Serves 6

BLACK TRUFFLE BUTTER
1 ounce fresh black truffles
1 tablespoon black truffle oil
1 stick European-style butter, softened
Salt, to taste
White pepper, to taste

FAVA BEANS
½ cup fava beans

SMOKED-SALT FINGERLING POTATOES
5 medium fingerling potatoes
¼ cup duck fat, rendered
½ teaspoon Yakima smoked sea salt

TOMATO CONFIT
1 cup extra-virgin olive oil
½ cup cherry tomatoes
Salt, to taste

GROUPER
6 (7-ounce) black grouper fillets
Salt, to taste
White pepper, to taste
¼ cup extra-virgin olive oil
2 cups oyster mushrooms, cleaned
1 teaspoon garlic, sliced
½ cup white wine
½ cup Fish Fumet (page 209)
½ teaspoon fresh thyme leaves
1 tablespoon Italian parsley, chopped
Black Truffle Butter (see above)

FOR ASSEMBLY
1 ounce fresh black truffle, shaved
Black truffle oil

PREPARE BLACK TRUFFLE BUTTER
Place all ingredients in a food processor and blend until smooth. Refrigerate until needed.

PREPARE FAVA BEANS
Shell fava beans and blanch in salted boiling water for 1 to 2 minutes. Drain and place in ice water. Drain and remove second shells from fava beans.

PREPARE SMOKED-SALT FINGERLING POTATOES
Steam potatoes for 20 to 25 minutes over boiling water. Cool completely. Slice in ½- to ¾-inch coins. In a sauté pan over medium heat, place rendered duck fat and potato coins. Cook each side for 2 minutes or until golden brown. Finish with smoked salt.

PREPARE TOMATO CONFIT
Bring oil to 350°F in a large saucepot over medium-high heat. Add cherry tomatoes and partly cover with a lid, avoiding splashing or popping oil. Cook for 1 to 2 minutes. Drain tomatoes with a metal strainer and lay on a towel to remove excess oil. Season to taste.

PREPARE GROUPER
Preheat oven to 375°F. Season fish to taste. Divide oil between 2 large sauté pans set over medium-high heat. Add fish and sear until golden brown, about 3 minutes. Flip fish and divide mushrooms and garlic among each pan. Deglaze with wine and fish fumet. Transfer pans to oven and bake for 8 to 10 minutes, until fish is cooked through. Remove from oven and return pans to the stovetop. Reduce remaining liquid by two-thirds. Add fava beans, potatoes, tomatoes, thyme, black truffle butter and parsley. Reduce to a creamy consistency.

ASSEMBLE
Divide fish-cooking sauce among 6 plates. Add fish fillets over sauce. Top fish with black truffle shavings and finish with a drizzle of black truffle oil.

BLACK COD FILLET WITH BLACK TRUFFLE, SERRANO HAM, FIGS AND AMARONE ZABAGLIONE

Sometimes when I create a new dish I like to take a small trip in my mind. This one takes me to my childhood home in Venice, where you find all of these ingredients—even the Spanish Serrano ham uses a curing method from way back in the day. This dish becomes a nostalgic trip of flavor for my mouth.

Serves 6

SERRANO HAM MARBLE
12 slices Serrano ham, paper thin

STRAWBERRY JUICE
1 cup strawberries, stemmed
2 teaspoons lemon juice
1 tablespoon sugar
¼ cup cold water

FISH
6 (7-ounce) fillets black cod
Salt, to taste
Freshly ground black pepper, to taste
1 tablespoon butter
¾ ounce black truffles, shaved
2 sage leaves
¼ cup grapeseed oil

ZABAGLIONE SAUCE
2 egg yolks
1 tablespoon sugar
¼ cup Amarone wine
¼ cup Strawberry Juice (page 208)
White pepper, to taste
Salt, to taste

FOR ASSEMBLY
12 black mission figs, quartered
½ ounce microgreens
1 teaspoon lemon juice
¾ ounce black truffles, shaved
1 tablespoon black truffle oil mist

PREPARE SERRANO MARBLE
Shingle 2 slices ham on a piece of plastic wrap and cover with more wrap. Slice ham to make a 3 x 3–inch square. Repeat 5 times, making 6 servings.

PREPARE STRAWBERRY JUICE
Wash berries and dry in a towel. Place all ingredients in a blender and puree until smooth. Pass through a fine-mesh sieve.

PREPARE FISH
Bring a large pot of water to 140°F, adjusting heat level to maintain a constant temperature. Season fish to taste. Place black cod, butter, truffles and sage leaves in a vacuum bag and seal. Place bag in a water bath and cook fish for 35 minutes. Remove bag from water. Heat grapeseed oil in a sauté pan. Sear each piece of fish, presentation side down, for 30 seconds or until top turns golden. Remove from pan and reserve for plating.

PREPARE ZABAGLIONE SAUCE
Prepare a double boiler. In a metal mixing bowl, combine egg yolks, sugar, wine, strawberry juice, white pepper and salt. Place mixing bowl over the double boiler and cook, whisking constantly. Remove mixing bowl periodically so as not to overheat the mixture. Cook for 5 minutes or until zabaglione is frothy and soft peaks can form.

ASSEMBLE
Lay each Serrano ham marble on a plate, removing both sides of plastic wrap. Place black cod on top of the marble in center, seared side up. Arrange quartered figs around fish. Top fish with a dollop of Amarone zabaglione. Toss microgreens with lemon juice and scatter among plates. Distribute black truffle shavings over fish and spray with black truffle mist.

DUCK FAT-POACHED AHI TUNA WITH ORANGE MOSCATO NECTAR, FOIE GRAS STRACCIATELLA, SALSIFY PUREE

Poaching the tuna in duck fat lends an extra richness and depth of flavor to the fish. We marinate the foie gras to add some sweetness, then shave it like a truffle. It melts as soon as it touches the plate, adding a truly magical flavor. Combine with orange nectar and delicate sour from the stracciatella. It is truly a sophisticated tuna.

Serves 6

FOIE GRAS

6 ounces foie gras, Grade A
½ teaspoon sugar
½ teaspoon pink curing salt
Black pepper, to taste
1 tablespoon Moscato wine

SALSIFY PUREE

1 pound salsify, peeled
¼ cup Roasted Pears (page 212), chopped
1 tablespoon mascarpone cheese
1 teaspoon honey
½ cup Chicken Stock (page 209)
3 tablespoons extra-virgin olive oil
Salt, to taste
Freshly ground black pepper, to taste

ORANGE MOSCATO SAUCE

4 cups orange juice
1 cup Moscato wine
½ tablespoon sugar
Salt, to taste
2 tablespoon grapeseed oil
2 tablespoons extra-virgin olive oil

TUNA

6 cups duck fat
6 (7-ounce) tuna steaks, each 1-inch thick
Salt, to taste
Freshly ground black pepper, to taste

FOR ASSEMBLY

5 ounces stracciatella cheese
1 teaspoon Murray River salt

PREPARE FOIE GRAS

Combine all ingredients in a Cryovac bag and seal. Refrigerate bag for 10 hours. Remove foie gras from liquid. Place inside a clean Cryovac bag and seal. Let rest in freezer until frozen.

PREPARE SALSIFY PURÉE

Boil salsify in a small saucepot until tender, 25 to 30 minutes, depending on the thickness of the root. Chop into large chunks and place in a saucepot along with pears, mascarpone, honey, stock and 1 tablespoon oil. Season and cook for 4 minutes. Transfer to a blender and puree with remaining oil, adding more stock if needed. Keep warm.

PREPARE ORANGE MOSCATO SAUCE

Simmer juice, wine and sugar in a saucepan until reduced by half. Season mixture and transfer to a blender. With blender running, add oils a little at a time so the sauce emulsifies. Set aside.

PREPARE TUNA

Bring duck fat to 140°F in a large saucepot over medium heat. Season tuna and place in fat. Cook for 5 minutes, until rare. Remove tuna with a slotted spoon and dry excess fat with paper towels.

ASSEMBLE

Ladle orange Moscato sauce over 6 plates. Place 1 scoop salsify purée onto each plate. Slice each tuna fillet into 5 pieces on top of salsify. Sprinkle Murray River salt over each piece. Scatter stracciatella around the plate. Shave frozen foie gras with a mandoline on top of tuna.

MONKFISH AND CORN PUDDING WITH EGGPLANT, ASPARAGUS AND MORELS

Monkfish is considered "the poor man's lobster." When I was a kid, I would eat most of my seafood with polenta. To give it a different twist, I stepped it up a bit with corn pudding for an even creamier, richer flavor. Then the Venetian eggplant—oh, it's my favorite vegetable when I go there. But we even do that a little differently. We scoop out most of the pulp and cook the skin in olive oil and garlic—so wonderful and tender!

Serves 6

MONKFISH

6 (7-ounce) pieces monkfish, bone in
3 cloves garlic, peeled and mashed
1 tablespoon extra virgin olive oil
1 tablespoon canola oil
3 sprigs fresh rosemary
½ cup dry white wine
Sea salt, to taste
White pepper, to taste

EGGPLANT

3 (1-1½ pounds each) eggplants
3 cloves garlic, peeled and thinly sliced
3 tablespoons extra-virgin olive oil
½ cup Chicken Stock (page 209)
Sea salt, to taste
Freshly ground black pepper, to taste

CORN PUDDING

2 tablespoons extra-virgin olive oil
1 shallot, peeled and finely chopped
3 ears fresh corn, roasted and kernels removed
1 tablespoon tequila
1½ cups heavy cream
2 tablespoons grade A honey
1 tablespoon white sugar
1 tablespoon unsalted butter
Sea salt, to taste
Freshly ground black pepper, to taste

ASPARAGUS AND MORELS

18 fresh asparagus stalks
18 fresh morel mushrooms, as similar in size as possible
1 shallot, peeled and finely chopped
2 tablespoons extra-virgin olive oil
1 tablespoon flat-leaf parsley, chopped
1 tablespoon unsalted butter
Sea salt, to taste
Freshly ground black pepper, to taste

MAKE EGGPLANT

Trim about ½ inch from each end of eggplant. Place trimmed eggplant upright and slice skin downward in even strips about ¼ inch thick by 2 inches wide. Heat olive oil over medium heat in a large sauté pan. Add garlic, cooking briefly to a light golden color, then add eggplant strips and chicken stock. Cover and cook until tender, about 7 to 10 minutes. Season to taste and set aside.

MAKE CORN PUDDING

Heat olive oil in a saucepan over medium heat and sauté shallot for about 2 minutes, stirring frequently to prevent burning. Add roasted-corn kernels and tequila and cook for a few minutes more. Add cream, honey and sugar and bring to a boil. Lower heat to a simmer and cook 3 to 4 minutes more, stirring occasionally. Pour corn mixture into a blender, or the bowl of the food processor, and puree for about 1 minute. Strain corn mixture using a sieve over a large bowl, pressing mixture through the mesh with a spatula. Pour strained mixture back into the saucepan and add butter. Cook over medium-high heat, stirring frequently, for a few minutes to reach a smooth consistency. Remove from heat and set aside.

PREPARE ASPARAGUS AND MORELS

Clean morels by soaking briefly in cool water then gently rinsing. (You may need to wash them twice as the grooves in the cap tend to hold bits of dirt.) Gently pat dry using paper towels.

Trim asparagus tips to 3-inch lengths, discarding stalks. Steam asparagus tips until just tender, about 3 minutes, then chill in an ice bath to prevent further cooking.

Heat olive oil in a sauté pan over medium heat and cook shallot for few minutes, stirring occasionally. Add morels and cook 3 to 4 minutes. Add parsley, butter and asparagus tips, cooking until asparagus is warmed through. Season to taste. Remove from heat and set aside, uncovered.

PREPARE MONKFISH

Season monkfish to taste. In a sauté pan, add canola oil and heat. Add rosemary, garlic and fish. Flip the fillets, splash with white wine and bake in the oven at 400°F for 6 to 7 minutes.

FINISH MONKFISH

Warm 6 plates and spread a small portion of corn pudding into the center of each plate. Spoon some eggplant over pudding and top with 1 fish fillet. Arrange asparagus and morels, adding the juice from the pan around the fish. Then drizzle with a little olive oil and the pan drippings from the monkfish. Serve.

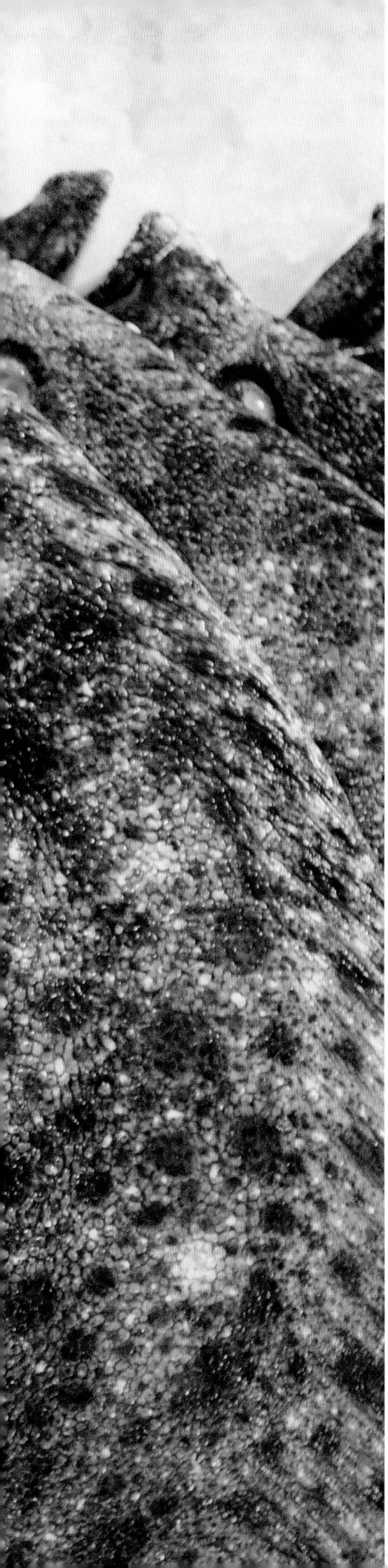

THE FISH LADY

Seafood Concierge

I knew when I met Susan Bulifant that we were going to be a match made in seafood heaven. The owner since 2006 of the Fish Lady, a very selective specialty-seafood wholesale company, Susan understands chefs—especially picky chefs like me.

She started in the seafood business in 1987 as a sales person, selling to European and other highly trained chefs who at the time were populating the best kitchens in Sanibel, Captiva and Naples. She learned about the importance of freshness and quality from the crème de la crème.

So Susan was not in the least bit intimidated by my high expectations and demands for excellence. She opened the Fish Lady specifically to cater to the custom needs of chefs who know what they want and want to serve their customers the best. She understood that, coming from a Venetian upbringing, I am accustomed to only the freshest fish. I want a specific species. I want it a certain size. I want it a certain cut. And whenever possible I even want to know what boat caught it, where and when. The more I can tell my customer about the fish he or she is eating, the more they are going to enjoy it and appreciate it.

If my executive chef, Jason, or I learn something new about a certain type of seafood, we can call the Fish Lady and Susan's staff of about 15 will track it down, exactly to our specifications.

She also knows what seafood to reserve for me whenever she finds rarities. For instance, it is difficult these days to find local wild-caught shrimp. The shrimpers on Pine Island bring in good-sized wild shrimp on a sporadic basis. Susan's relationships with her shrimpers allows her to buy up their catch almost exclusively for us.

She is kind of like a fish concierge that way. For imported seafood, she works closely with a few select vendors whom she has come to trust over the years. In this business, you look for honesty along with freshness. It's an unsteady market constantly affected by weather, the environment, overfishing and the integrity of the people in the business. Susan is very people-savvy and, as are we, sensitive to the sustainability of species.

Susan and her crew work as hard as we do at doing our best. Her workers come in at midnight to make sure the fish is cut the same day it gets delivered. She designs her schedule according to what we need and when, not what's convenient for her drivers. She's almost like one of our staff.

Susan always tells me, "Fabrizio, if your customers are happy, you are happy, and I am happy." Happiness rolls uphill.

MEAT
AND POULTRY

MEAT

Of Flavor and Protein

‡

My aunt in Italy always brought a chicken from her backyard whenever she came to visit us. Occasionally, we would have rabbit, but most often it was pork or pheasant. Beef was a luxury.

We buy five different types of beef for our restaurants. I don't mean five cuts, but five different varieties that we purchase from local U.S. farmers and abroad. Each variety tastes different and affects you, the diner, differently. For example, the Akaushi beef we buy from Clewiston, Florida, has the richest possible nutritional value. It makes you feel stronger after you eat it. And our grass-fed beef is a protein power.

People like their prime meat with lots of wonderful marbled fat that adds richness, like the fat in foie gras. It has so much flavor.

We dry- or wet-age some of our beef for 21 to 28 days in a salt cave made of Himalayan pink salt, so the meat gets almost a cured flavor, something of a signature for us. You can get a taste of it with the salt cave–aged rib-eye recipe.

In this chapter, I combine meat and salt in another way also, and that's with a sea salt brine. Now, if you're thinking that meat and salt are both bad for you, please understand that both have very healthful properties.

Meat is, of course, an important source of protein, but like anything it should be consumed in moderation. I always say if you're going to eat meat, eat the best you can afford. Then eat poultry and no-meat dishes to balance your red meat intake.

You will also find one of my favorite home-cooked meals in this chapter—a chicken dish I have been eating since I was a little boy. It's true comfort food for me, and I never grow tired of its folky heartiness.

AKAUSHI BEEF TENDERLOIN WITH ASPARAGUS, MORELS AND RED PEPPER-DATE SAUCE

Akaushi means "red cow." It is a Japanese Wagyu breed of cattle with beautiful marbling. It is healthier because of its fatty acid composition when compared to other domestic beef and is also exceptionally tender, juicy and flavorful.

Serves 6

DATE SAUCE

3 cups Barhi dates
1 cup port wine
1 cup white balsamic vinegar
1 cup Beef Stock (page 208)
¼ cup sugar
1 cinnamon stick
4 whole allspice berries
3 black peppercorns
2 whole cloves
2 juniper berries, slightly crushed
2 teaspoons orange zest
2 teaspoons lemon zest
Sea salt, to taste
6 ounces Roasted Bell Peppers (page 212), cut into 1-inch squares

ASPARAGUS AND MORELS

18 stems asparagus
18 medium morel mushrooms
⅓ cup olive oil
Sea salt, to taste
Freshly ground black pepper, to taste

TENDERLOIN

6 (6-ounce) Akaushi beef tenderloins, trimmed
Sea salt, to taste
Freshly ground black pepper, to taste
½ cup grapeseed oil
7 garlic cloves, peeled and crushed
2 (5-inch) springs fresh rosemary

PREPARE DATE SAUCE

In a medium saucepan, stir together dates, port, vinegar, stock, sugar, cinnamon stick, allspice, peppercorns, cloves, juniper berries and zests. Cook over medium heat until liquid is reduced by one-third. Stir in salt. Pass through a fine-mesh sieve and return to a clean medium saucepan. Over medium heat, reduce by half again until the sauce starts to thicken. Remove from heat, add red bell peppers and set aside. (You can make this ahead of time and reheat over low heat before serving.)

PREPARE ASPARAGUS AND MORELS

Boil salted water in a pot large enough to hold the asparagus. Meanwhile, prepare an ice bath by adding cold water and ice cubes to a large bowl. Blanch asparagus in boiling water for 3 minutes or until tender. Chill rapidly in ice bath, then remove and pat dry with paper towels.
To trim the asparagus, cut 2 inches off the tip, and set aside. Stuff stem end of each stalk into a morel. Heat olive oil in a medium sauté pan over medium-high heat. Sauté asparagus and morels until golden brown, about 3 to 4 minutes. Season to taste.

PREPARE STEAK

Season beef tenderloins to taste. In a large sauté skillet, heat oil over medium-high heat until shimmering. Quickly sear all sides of the tenderloins. Add garlic cloves and rosemary. Lower heat to medium and continue cooking until meat is desired temperature. Turn meat and garlic frequently for even doneness.

ASSEMBLE

Arrange each tenderloin on a plate. Spoon sauce around the tenderloin and place asparagus tips and asparagus-morel combos to the side.

BRINED KUROBUTA PORK CHOPS WITH BLACK CHERRY SAUCE AND SUMMER VEGETABLES

As the story goes, England made a gift of Berkshire hogs to Japan. What resulted is the beautifully marbled Kurobuta pork. Black cherry, with a touch of licorice flavor, makes a nice, sweet complement. Just make sure you don't overcook the pork.

Serves 6

BLACK CHERRY SAUCE

½ cup guanciale (or pancetta or bacon), diced
3 cups Chicken Stock (page 209)
1 cup port wine
½ cup balsamic vinegar
1 tablespoon Pernod
2 tablespoons beet juice
3 pods star anise
1 cup sugar
1 quart fresh (or frozen) black cherries, pitted
Sea salt, to taste
¼ cup butter, room temperature, cut into pieces

SUMMER VEGETABLES

18 baby carrots
30 snow peas, strings removed
30 green pea pods, strings removed
12 pieces fresh (or frozen) baby corn-on-the-cob
1 tablespoon olive oil
18 date (or grape) tomatoes
Sea salt, to taste

PORK CHOPS

6 (12-ounce) French-boned Kurobuta pork chops, brined for 7-8 hours (Meat and Poultry Brine, page 208)
Sea salt, to taste
Freshly ground black pepper, to taste
2 tablespoon grapeseed (or canola) oil
1 (5-inch) fresh rosemary sprig
6 garlic cloves, peeled and crushed
2 tablespoons butter
3 ounces Pistachio Paste (page 211)

PREPARE SAUCE

Heat a large saucepan over medium-high heat. When hot, add guanciale and cook, for about 3 minutes. Add chicken stock, port wine, balsamic vinegar, Pernod, beet juice, star anise and sugar. Stir well and bring to a low boil. Reduce heat to low and simmer, covered, for 1 hour. Add half the cherries. Return to a simmer and continue to cook another 30 minutes, uncovered. Remove pan from burner and stir in remaining cherries. Remove anise pods. Add salt, to taste. Set aside. Before serving, add butter and stir until melted.

**Note: This tastes best when prepared a day ahead and refrigerated overnight. To use, reheat on low until warm.*

PREPARE VEGETABLES

Bring 2 quarts water to a boil in a medium pot. Add baby carrots and cook for 4 minutes. Add green peas, snow peas and corn. Cook for another 2 minutes or until the vegetables are al dente. While the vegetables finish cooking, heat olive oil in a large sauté pan over medium heat. Drain the cooked vegetables, toss into the pan, add tomatoes and sauté lightly for about 1 minute. Add sea salt to taste.

PREPARE PORK CHOPS

Remove chops from brine and pat dry. Salt and pepper both sides. Heat oil to shimmering in large skillet over medium-high heat. Place pork chops, rosemary and garlic in pan. Cook to desired doneness, about 5 minutes each side, turning garlic cloves to avoid burning. Swirl in butter and cook another 2 to 3 minutes.

ASSEMBLE

Divide pork chops among 6 plates. Top with cherry sauce and arrange vegetables on the side. Dot plate with pistachio paste.

DUCK BREAST WITH SEVRUGA CAVIAR, KUMAMOTO OYSTERS, CHIVE SOUR CREAM AND ROOTS

I think the best combination of flavors offers a taste of the land with a taste of the sea. The crispy duck skin with the salty caviar and oysters—mamma mia! It's the best of both worlds.

Serves 4

DUCK BREAST

4 muscovy duck breast halves, boned and skin on
2 cups coarse sea salt
4 tablespoons extra-virgin olive oil
2 tablespoons canola oil
3 sprigs fresh rosemary
3 sprigs fresh sage
3 sprigs fresh lavender
Freshly ground black pepper, to taste

OYSTERS

½ cup all-purpose flour
½ cup buttermilk
1 teaspoon flat-leaf parsley, finely chopped
1 cup canola oil
12 Kumamoto oysters, shucked
Sea salt, to taste
Freshly ground black pepper, to taste

CHIVE SOUR CREAM

½ cup sour cream
¼ cup heavy cream
2 tablespoons fresh chives, finely chopped

ROOT VEGETABLES

4 baby red beets, peeled
4 baby carrots, peeled
4 baby turnips, peeled
2 tablespoons extra-virgin olive oil
Sea salt, to taste
Freshly ground black pepper, to taste

FOR ASSEMBLY

2 ounces sevruga caviar
3 tablespoons Duck Jus (page 209)
2 tablespoons grade-A honey

PREPARE DUCK BREASTS

Trim excess fat from duck breasts, leaving skin on the top side of breasts. Using a knife, cut a crisscross pattern across skin. Place about 1 cup coarse sea salt onto baking sheet. Lay duck breasts skin side down on the salt. Cover with plastic wrap and let rest for 4 hours.

(While duck rests in salt, prepare the other ingredient lists for this dish.)

After 4 hours, remove duck breasts from salt and rinse well under cool water. Pat dry. Heat up sous-vide machine to 139°F. Place duck breasts and olive oil in a vacuum bag. Seal bag and cook sous vide for 40 minutes, maintaining a constant water temperature of 139°F. Remove duck breasts from bag.

Heat canola oil in a sauté pan over medium-high heat. Lay duck breasts, skin side down, in the pan. Add rosemary, sage and lavender and sear skin to a golden brown. Reduce heat, if necessary, to prevent burning. Turn over duck breasts to sear other side for 1 minute. Remove from pan, season with pepper and set aside.

ALTERNATE METHOD

Follow instructions above for preparing the duck. When breasts have been salted, rinsed and dried, preheat oven to 380°F. Heat canola oil in a sauté pan over medium-high heat. Lay duck breasts, skin side down, in the pan. Add rosemary, sage and lavender and sear skin to a golden brown. Reduce heat, if necessary, to prevent burning. Turn over duck breasts to sear other side for 1 minute. Transfer duck breasts to a baking sheet, skin side up. Finish cooking breasts in the oven for 10 minutes for medium rare, to an internal temperature of 135°F. Remove from oven, season with pepper and set aside.

PREPARE OYSTERS

Place flour in a small mixing bowl. In another small mixing bowl, combine buttermilk and parsley. Heat canola oil in a sauté pan over medium heat. Pat excess moisture off oysters with paper towels. Dip oysters, one at a time, first in flour, then in buttermilk mixture, and carefully drop into the hot oil. Cook for 1 minute, turning over halfway through cooking process. Transfer to paper towels to remove excess oil. Season to taste.

PREPARE SOUR CREAM

Combine all ingredients in a small mixing bowl and mix well. Cover and let rest in refrigerator.

PREPARE ROOT VEGETABLES

Preheat oven to 350°F. Wrap beets in foil and roast in the oven for 30 to 35 minutes, until tender, and then cut into quarters. Steam carrots and turnips over high heat for 6 to 8 minutes, until tender. Cut carrots into halves and turnips into quarters. Be careful not to overcook.

Combine carrots and turnips in a medium bowl. Place beets in another bowl (so the color doesn't bleed onto the other vegetables). Toss both with oil and season to taste.

ASSEMBLE

Warm 4 dinner plates. Thinly slice each duck breast. Spoon a few tablespoons sour cream onto the center of each plate, spreading slightly. Fan out duck breast slices on top of sour cream. Garnish each plate with ½ ounce caviar, spooning some onto each breast slice. Top with a drizzle of honey and a drizzle of duck jus. Divide root vegetables and oysters among the 4 plates. Serve.

VENISON TENDERLOIN WITH CHESTNUT GRAPPA SAUCE AND BRAISED ROOT VEGETABLES

I made this dish for the first time in our restaurant in Washington, D.C., for an Italian friend who loves grappa and venison, too. For winter, the chestnut sauce is perfect. It all came out of talking food and drinking grappa with friends.

Serves 6

BRINE

½ cup raspberry vinegar
½ cup balsamic vinegar
1 tablespoon gin
4 cups water
1 cup sea salt
1 tablespoon black peppercorns
1 cup brown sugar
1 tablespoon coriander seeds
3 tablespoons juniper berries, slightly crushed
6 bay leaves
2 heads garlic, cut crosswise
10 cups ice cubes

VENISON

3 venison tenderloins
3 tablespoons extra-virgin olive oil
6 (5-inch) sprigs fresh rosemary

CHESTNUT CONFIT

3 cup water
1 cup sugar
2 (5-inch) sprigs rosemary
1 cup fresh (or frozen) chestnuts, peeled

CHESTNUT SAUCE

1 cup Chestnut Confit (see above)
2 cups Venison Glacé (page 213)
¼ cup chestnut syrup
2 tablespoons grappa

BRAISED VEGETABLES

18 baby turnips
2 tablespoons Grand Marnier
¼ cup white balsamic vinegar
1 tablespoon brown sugar
18 baby gold beets
18 baby carrots
1 celery root, cubed
1 quart Chicken Stock (page 209)
1 tablespoon black peppercorns
2 sprigs fresh thyme
2 tablespoons extra-virgin olive oil
2 tablespoons butter
½ tablespoon sea salt
½ teaspoon freshly ground black pepper

PREPARE VENISON

Combine all ingredients except ice cubes in a pot. Bring to a boil and simmer for 5 minutes. Add ice cubes to cool. Submerge tenderloins in brine and let sit in refrigerator for 6 hours.

PREPARE CHESTNUT CONFIT

In a small saucepan, combine water, sugar and rosemary and bring to a boil. Lower heat to a simmer and cook until a syrupy consistency. Gently stir in chestnuts and simmer until tender but firm. Remove rosemary sprigs.

MAKE CHESTNUT SAUCE

Combine confit, glacé and syrup. Bring to a simmer and cook for 3 minutes. Add grappa and cook for 1 to 2 minutes.

FINISH VENISON

Remove venison from brine and towel dry. Place in a Cryovac bag. Add olive oil and rosemary and seal. Cook sous vide at 135°F for 45 minutes. Remove from bag. In a large sauté pan over high heat, sear all sides of tenderloins. (If not preparing by sous vide method, simply pan-sear venison over medium-high heat to desired internal temperature, 6 to 7 minutes.) Remove from pan and set aside.

PREPARE VEGETABLES

Preheat oven to 350°F. Peel and trim turnips, leaving 1 inch of stem. In a 2-quart casserole dish, combine Grand Marnier, vinegar and brown sugar. Add turnips, beets, carrots, celery root, stock, peppercorns and thyme. Stir well. Cover and bake until vegetables are tender, up to 1 hour. Remove from oven and drain.

In a sauté pan over medium-high heat, place oil, butter and braised vegetables. Stir occasionally to evenly caramelize, cooking for about 5 minutes. Season to taste.

ASSEMBLE

Sauce 6 plates, then add vegetables. Cut each tenderloin into 2 medallions and place 1 medallion over vegetables on each plate. Serve.

BEST CHICKEN EVER 'NILDE'

Cooking is not my wife, Ingrid's, strong suit. (Sorry, Darling, but it's true.) This wonderful, rustic dish was a specialty of my Aunt Nilde's in Italy, and it happens to be one of the only dinners Ingrid enjoys making—and prepares exceptionally well. We eat it at home often and every bite reminds me of my childhood.

Serves 6

2 (2½-pound) whole free-range chickens, cut into 12 pieces
½ cup olive oil
Sea salt, to taste
Freshly ground black pepper, to taste
7 garlic cloves, peeled and sliced
2 medium green bell peppers, seeded and cut into ⅜-inch squares
2 medium red bell peppers, seeded and cut into ⅜-inch squares
2 (6-inch) fresh rosemary sprigs
1½ cups kalamata (or other) Greek olives
¾ cup sun-dried tomatoes in oil, each cut in half
1 cup Chicken Stock (page 209)

PROCEDURE

Cut each chicken into 12 parts—drumsticks, thighs, wings and 6 breast pieces. Save neck and back for Chicken Stock (page 209).

Heat oil in a large skillet (use 2 skillets, if necessary) over medium-high heat until it shimmers. Add chicken. As it cooks, toss in salt, pepper, garlic, peppers and rosemary, stirring them into oil. Cook for 10 minutes. Add black olives and sun-dried tomatoes. Stir for 3 minutes, then add chicken stock. Cover pan with lid slightly ajar so steam can escape. Lower heat to medium and continue cooking for 30 to 35 minutes or until the meat falls off the bone.

If liquid level gets too low during cooking, add additional stock or water. If too watery when chicken is done, remove chicken from skillet and simmer until sauce reaches desired consistency.

Remove rosemary sprigs. Serve family-style with a loaf of rustic bread for dipping.

GUINEA HEN WITH BLACK GARLIC, EGG YOLK TRUFFLE AND APRICOT SAUCE

Guinea hens are native to Africa and were raised by the ancient Egyptians. These birds have had a history of culinary regard since 2400 BC. This is the mildest of the game birds, its flavor closest to chicken, with a subtle punch and pleasant complexity.

Serves 6

EGG YOLK TRUFFLE
7 whole eggs
2 teaspoons water, room temperature
1 cup all-purpose flour
1 cup very fine breadcrumbs
Sea salt, to taste
2 cups grapeseed oil, for frying

SAUCE
½ tablespoon butter
1 teaspoon fresh rosemary leaves, chopped
1 tablespoon extra-virgin olive oil
¾ cup dried apricots, halved
1 teaspoon brown sugar
Pinch saffron threads
1 tablespoon apricot liqueur
1 tablespoon white balsamic vinegar
1 cup Veal Jus (page 212)
1½ cups Chicken Stock (page 209)
2 bay leaves
¼ teaspoon ground cumin
Sea salt, to taste
Freshly ground black pepper, to taste

ASPARAGUS
½ gallon cold water
Ice cubes
12 spears white asparagus, tips only
12 spears green asparagus, tips only
1 tablespoon olive oil
Sea salt, to taste

GUINEA HEN
6 guinea hen breasts, boneless, skin on and butterflied (wings on if desired)
4 ounces (3–4 bulbs) fermented black garlic
¼ cup olive oil, plus 3 tablespoons for sautéing, if cooking sous vide
¼ cup butter
3 (5-inch) sprigs fresh thyme
Sea salt, to taste
Freshly ground black pepper, to taste

PREPARE EGG YOLK TRUFFLE

Cook 6 whole eggs. Prepare a sous vide bath with 1 gallon water and bring to 147°F. Add eggs and cook for 45 minutes. Alternately, bring ½ gallon water to a boil in a medium saucepan. Add 6 eggs and cook for 5 to 6 minutes. Prepare an ice bath, add eggs and let cool for 5 minutes. Peel eggs, discarding whites and keeping yolks. If using sous vide method, return egg yolks to ice water.

Combine remaining egg and the water. Place egg wash, flour and breadcrumbs in separate deep bowls. Dip 1 cooked yolk in the flour, then the egg wash, and swirl to coat. Finally, roll yolk in breadcrumbs until completely coated. Season, to taste. Place yolk on a large plate. Repeat process with remaining yolks. Add oil to a 10-inch sauté pan over medium-high heat. When it reaches 370°F, add yolks, one at a time, deep-frying for 30 to 60 seconds. Remove from oil and drain on paper towels. Set truffles aside.

PREPARE SAUCE

Melt butter in a medium saucepan over medium-low heat. Add rosemary and oil and cook for 1 minute. Stir in apricots, brown sugar, saffron, liqueur and vinegar. Cook for 1½ minutes. Add veal jus, chicken stock, bay leaves and cumin. Simmer for 15 to 20 minutes, until sauce reaches a consistency that coats the back of the spoon. Remove bay leaves and season to taste.

PREPARE ASPARAGUS

Fill a pot large enough to hold asparagus with water and salt and bring to a boil. Meanwhile, prepare an ice bath, placing water and ice in a large bowl. Cook asparagus in boiling water for 3 to 4 minutes, then cool in ice water. Remove from bath and pat dry. Toss with oil, season and set aside.

PREPARE GUINEA HEN

Peel black garlic by slicing off the top of each bulb and pulling cloves apart. Remove peels. Cut thicker cloves in half lengthwise.

Open butterflied hen breasts. Stuff with garlic cloves and fold over. To cook sous vide, place breasts in Cryovac bags with oil, butter, thyme, salt and pepper in equal amounts among each bag. Vacuum seal and cook at 139°F for 45 minutes. Remove from bag. Place remaining oil in a sauté pan over high heat. When oil is hot, sear hen breasts, skin side down, until golden. Flip and sauté on opposite side for a few minutes. Repeat with remaining breasts.

Alternately, heat oil and butter in a frying pan over medium-high heat. Meanwhile, preheat oven to 385°F. Close open sides of hens with toothpicks. When pan is hot, add thyme and garlic-stuffed breasts, flipping once. Transfer breasts to oven and cook to an internal temperature of 180°F, about 15 minutes. Season to taste.

ASSEMBLE

Slice each hen breast diagonally into 3 pieces and place in the center of a plate. Arrange asparagus around the plate and add egg truffle. Finish with sauce and repeat for each serving.

SALT CAVE-AGED RIB-EYE STEAK WITH COCOA NIBS AND BACON–CELERY ROOT BRÛLÉE

Cocoa nibs, the crunchy state chocolate reaches as it is being processed, change the entire character of the beef in this dish. It's no longer that steak-and-fries slab of meat. It becomes a delicate dish that deserves a violinist and a cozy restaurant corner.

Serves 6

BACON–CELERY ROOT BRÛLÉE

2 tablespoons extra-virgin olive oil
1 shallot, thinly sliced
½ cup leeks, thinly sliced
½ cup celery root, thinly sliced
½ cup green apple, thinly sliced
Salt, to taste
White pepper, to taste
2 cups heavy cream
2 Kurobuta bacon slices, finely diced
6 egg yolks
1 tablespoon potato starch

CRISPY BACON

14 Kurobuta bacon slices
3 tablespoons butter
3 tablespoons brown sugar

SAUCE

3 tablespoons organic soy sauce
¼ cup Veal Jus (page 212)
2 tablespoons butter, cold and cut into small pieces

RIB-EYE

6 (7-ounce) salt cave-aged rib-eye fillets, just the eye of the rib-eye, without the spinalis
Coarsely ground black pepper, to taste
Salt, to taste
2 tablespoons extra-virgin olive oil
¾ cup cocoa nibs
2 tablespoons butter

FOR ASSEMBLY

2 tablespoons brown sugar

PREPARE BRÛLÉE

Preheat oven to 300°F. In a sauté pan over medium-high heat, place oil, shallot, leeks, celery root, green apple, salt and pepper. Cook, stirring occasionally, until the root vegetables have sweated, about 5 minutes. Add heavy cream and bring to a boil. Simmer for 3 to 4 minutes. Remove from heat and puree in a blender until smooth. Strain cream mixture through a chinois into a medium-size saucepan. Over medium-high heat, whisk in diced bacon and egg yolks, then reduce heat to medium, taking care to maintain a simmer. Place potato starch and a little water into a small bowl and stir to dissolve. Mix potato starch into the saucepan, whisking continuously until achieving a light, pudding-like consistency.

Remove from heat and divide equally among 6 (8-ounce) ramekins. Place them in a 9 x 13-inch cake pan and add enough hot water so the ramekins are submerged one-third of the way up. Cover pan with aluminum foil and bake for 20 to 30 minutes, until the centers have set. Remove from the oven and the water bath, and refrigerate ramekins until brûlées are firm.

PREPARE BACON

Preheat oven to 400°F. Finely chop 2 bacon slices and place in a food processor with the butter and brown sugar. Purée until creamy. Place 6 bacon slices on a parchment paper-lined baking sheet. Spread half the pureed bacon over the bacon slices and top each with another bacon slice. Spread remaining mixture over the top of the bacon stacks. Cover with parchment paper and weigh down with a second baking sheet, then weigh down the second baking sheet with a 9 x 13-inch baking pan half-full of water. Bake for 15 to 20 minutes, until bacon is crispy. Remove each bacon stack, pat dry with a paper towel, and set aside.

PREPARE SAUCE

Place soy sauce in a saucepot and bring to a boil. Add jus and bring back to a boil. Remove from heat and whisk in butter. Keep warm but do not boil or butter will separate.

PREPARE RIB-EYE

Place rib-eye fillets on a plate and season to taste. Drizzle tops with oil. Place a cast-iron pan over medium-high heat, add fillets and sear for 2 minutes on each side, or to desired doneness. Let meat rest in the pan. Mix cocoa nibs and butter in a small bowl and spread equally among the steaks. Place the pan under the broiler for less than a minute, just to melt the butter. Take care not to burn the cocoa nibs.

ASSEMBLE

Warm brûlées in the microwave for 20 seconds. Sprinkle with brown sugar and use a blowtorch to caramelize the tops. On each plate, place rib-eye fillet on one side and brûlée on the other. Place 1 bacon slice between the meat and brûlée. Drizzle sauce on top of meat.

RACK OF LAMB WITH PEPPERMINT EMULSION, ROSEMARY JUICE, PURPLE POTATO AND BRUSSELS LEAVES

The first time I ate lamb with mint jelly was here in the U.S. Now I love the combination, however traditions have changed since then. Today you're more likely to find lamb with a mustard crust. With this recipe I wanted to bring back that mint jelly nostalgia but in a new, refined way.

Serves 4

PEPPERMINT EMULSION

2 egg yolks
Salt, to taste
1 tablespoon lemon juice
¾ cup extra-virgin olive oil
1 tablespoon green peppermint extract

MINTED POTATOES

12 small Peruvian potatoes
Salt, to taste
White pepper, to taste
1 tablespoon extra-virgin olive oil
8 mint leaves, thinly sliced

ROSEMARY JUICE

1 tablespoon fresh rosemary leaves, chopped
¼ cup red wine
½ cup lamb jus
Salt, to taste
Freshly ground black pepper, to taste

BRUSSELS SPROUT LEAVES

4 Brussels sprouts
Salt, to taste
1 tablespoon extra-virgin olive oil

LAMB

2 whole racks of lamb, Frenched
Salt, to taste
Freshly ground black pepper, to taste
1 tablespoon extra-virgin olive oil
1 tablespoon canola oil
3 sprigs fresh rosemary
2 sprigs fresh sage

FOR ASSEMBLY

1 teaspoon Murray River salt
Freshly ground black pepper, to taste

PREPARE PEPPERMINT EMULSION

In a bowl, using a hand mixer, quickly combine egg yolks, salt and lemon juice. Add ¾ cup olive oil, a little at a time, in a thin, steady stream. Mix continuously until a soft mayonnaise-like consistency is achieved. Add peppermint extract and a little water if too thick. Set aside.

PREPARE MINTED POTATOES

Peel potatoes with a small paring knife into 2-inch-long seven-sided barrel shapes. (This technique is called tournéeing.) Boil them in salted water until cooked through. Drain and place in a mixing bowl. Add salt, pepper, extra-virgin olive oil and mint leaves and mix thoroughly. Keep warm.

PREPARE ROSEMARY JUICE

Blanche rosemary leaves in boiling water for 10 seconds. Drain and squeeze to remove the water. Place red wine and rosemary in a saucepan and reduce by half. Add lamb jus, salt and pepper and keep warm.

PREPARE BRUSSELS SPROUTS

Using a paring knife, core Brussels sprouts and separate leaves. Steam leaves over boiling water for 15 minutes to wilt them. Place in a small bowl and dress with salt and olive oil. Set aside.

PREPARE LAMB

Preheat oven to 400°F. Remove excess fat from lamb and season to taste. Add olive and canola oils to a cast-iron skillet and sear lamb over high heat. Transfer lamb to a roasting pan, add rosemary and sage and roast in the oven for 8 to 14 minutes, to your desired temperature. Remove from the oven and let rest for a few minutes.

ASSEMBLE

Slice 2 racks into 8 pieces and divide among 4 plates. Add 1 tablespoon peppermint emulsion and drag across each plate decoratively. Drizzle rosemary juice and arrange potatoes and Brussels sprout leaves around the lamb racks. Finish with Murray River salt and pepper, to taste.

BAR SANDWICHES

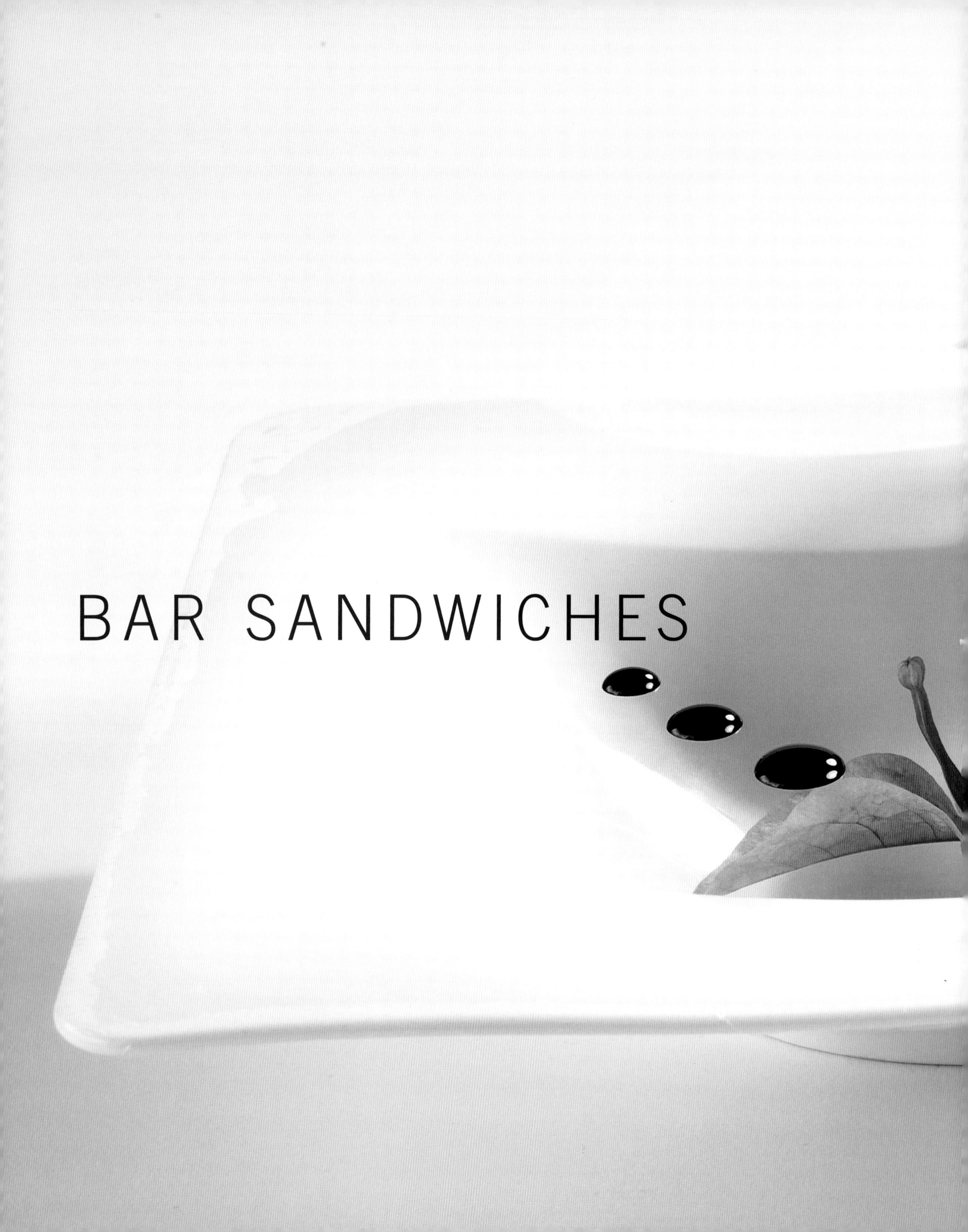

FIT FOR CHEFS

Compact Little Masterpieces

‡

Sometimes I think sandwiches were made for chefs. We rarely have time to sit down for a normal lunch or dinner. Even if we try, we're jumping up every two minutes to take care of something in the restaurant.

So at work, most of the time, I end up having a sandwich. Not only is it quick, but a sandwich is ultimately satisfying. And it doesn't have to be fancy or complicated. I love a very simple sandwich of warm bread with just fresh mozzarella or prosciutto.

The sandwiches we serve on our bar menu are a little more complex than that, though. We create them basically for ourselves. We aim to make our sandwiches different and delicious, so we just take a look at what we have fresh on the line and do some creative inventing.

For example, we give our customers an option of a kobe burger wrapped in iceberg lettuce instead of bread. I don't like a lot of thick bread with my sandwiches. I prefer thin bread so you can taste the filling and not feel too full.

Take our lobster reuben, for example. The first time I had one was in the Florida Keys, but the flavor of the lobster was so hidden by the breading and the big bun. So I decided to make mine truly like a reuben—grilled on thin bread with steamed lobster, house-made thousand island dressing and good sauerkraut. It became so popular that every time we tried to take it off the menu, our customers would protest.

You want the main attraction in your sandwich to stand out, but creative, well-made condiments are important and should complement rather than smother the taste, like the tomato-red onion marmalade on our grouper slider and jalapeño-red cabbage slaw on the crunchy chicken.

When you are serving sandwiches to guests, take the time to envision different accompaniments. You can turn a sandwich into a masterpiece with only a little effort.

BREAD LEAVES WITH PROSCIUTTO, PECORINO AND ARUGULA

1 loaf ciabatta bread, partially frozen
2 teaspoons extra-virgin olive oil, plus more for oiling bread
1 cup baby arugula leaves
1 teaspoon lemon juice
Sea salt, to taste
6 ounces prosciutto di Parma, shaved
3 ounces Pecorino Romano cheese, shaved
Good-quality aged balsamic vinegar
Freshly ground black pepper, to taste

PROCEDURE

Preheat oven to 350°F. Using a mandoline or very sharp knife, cut across the width of the bread, make 16 slices (bread leaves) no more than ¼-inch thick. Lay out bread leaves on baking tray. Brush each one with olive oil and bake for 4 to 6 minutes, until lightly golden. Set aside to cool.

In a small bowl, toss arugula with lemon juice, oil and a pinch of salt. Lay out 8 bread leaves on a clean surface. Top each with 2 slices prosciutto, arugula and some shaved Pecorino. Sprinkle each leaf with aged balsamic vinegar some black pepper. Top off bread leaf sandwiches with remaining 8 bread leaves.

FRIED GROUPER WITH TOMATO–RED ONION MARMALADE AND PICKLED CELERY

PICKLED CELERY

4 stalks celery, leaves trimmed, cut into 3 x ½-inch sticks
1 cup water
1 cup white vinegar
2 tablespoon white sugar
2 teaspoons salt
2 tablespoon pickling spices

TARTAR SAUCE

2 hard-boiled eggs, cooled, shelled and finely chopped
½ cup Mayonnaise (page 210)
2 tablespoons Vidalia onion, finely chopped
2 tablespoons roasted corn
1 tablespoon capers, chopped
1 teaspoon fresh jalapeño, seeded and finely chopped
½ teaspoon fresh cilantro, chopped
½ teaspoon tequila
½ teaspoon lemon juice
½ teaspoon lime juice

FRIED GROUPER

Tempura Batter:
¼ cup all-purpose flour
¼ cup rice flour
½ cup beer
½ teaspoon sea salt
4 (4–5 ounce) black grouper fillets
Oil, for frying, enough to submerge fish in pan
½ cup all-purpose flour, for dredging

FOR ASSEMBLY

4 (3½-4-inch) brioche buns
Tomato Marmalade (page 212)
1 ounce microgreens

PREPARE PICKLED CELERY

Bring water, vinegar, sugar, salt and spices to a boil. Reduce heat and simmer for 5 minutes. Remove from heat and let cool for 15 minutes. Strain out solids and pour liquid over celery so that the celery is completely submerged in the liquid. Refrigerate until cold, up to 24 hours, in a covered container.

PREPARE TARTAR SAUCE

Combine all ingredients in a bowl, mixing well. Season to taste. Cover with plastic wrap and refrigerate until ready to use.

PREPARE GROUPER

Whisk together all ingredients for the tempura batter in a bowl, creating a smooth batter. Heat oil in a heavy-bottomed stockpot or frying pan to 350°F. Dredge grouper fillets in flour, then dip in tempura batter. Fry for 4 to 6 minutes, turning over halfway through the cooking process. Fish is done when golden brown or internal temperature reaches 165°F. Drain fish on paper towels.

ASSEMBLE

Open brioche bun and spread bottom half with tartar sauce. Top with a piece of fish and spread fillet with some tomato marmalade. Add microgreens, pickled celery, and then top with other half of bun. Serve.

CRUNCHY CHICKEN WITH JALAPEÑO CABBAGE SLAW, SAFFRON AIOLI AND SRIRACHA MAYO

JALAPEÑO RED CABBAGE SLAW

2 cups red cabbage, thinly sliced
3 jalapeños, seeded and thinly sliced
1 small carrot, cut into julienne strips
2 tablespoons fresh cilantro, chopped
1 teaspoon honey
2 tablespoons sesame oil
2 tablespoons rice wine vinegar

SAFFRON AIOLI

1½ cups water
12 cloves garlic, peeled
¼ cup sugar
4 pinches saffron
1 teaspoon lemon juice
3 egg yolks
2 cups extra-virgin olive oil
Sea salt, to taste

SRIRACHA MAYO

½ cup Mayonnaise (page 210)
¼ cup ketchup
¼ cup Sriracha

CRUNCHY CHICKEN

4 (5–6 ounces) chicken breast halves, thinly pounded
Canola (or vegetable) oil, for frying
1 cup all-purpose flour
1 cup corn flour (harina de maiz, found in Spanish food section of grocery store)
1 teaspoon sea salt
2 cups buttermilk

FOR ASSEMBLY

4 (3½–4 inch) brioche buns, cut in half and toasted on grill or griddle

PREPARE SLAW

Combine all ingredients in a large bowl. Stir in oil and vinegar. Set aside.

PREPARE SAFFRON AIOLI

In a small saucepan, bring water, garlic, sugar and saffron to a boil. Lower heat and simmer for 10 to 12 minutes. Remove from heat and let cool completely. Reserve 3 tablespoons cooking liquid and all 12 garlic cloves.

In the bowl of a food processor, place reserved cooking liquid, lemon juice, garlic cloves and yolks. Puree, slowly adding olive oil to emulsify. Mixture will be slightly thick and fluffy. Add water, if necessary. Season to taste. Cover and set aside.

PREPARE SRIRACHA MAYO

Whisk together all ingredients in a small bowl. Cover and set aside.

PREPARE CHICKEN

Heat oil to 350°F in a heavy-bottomed stockpot or in a frying pan with tall sides. Meanwhile, combine flours and salt in a bowl. Pour buttermilk into a flat-bottomed, shallow baking dish. Dip breasts, one at a time, into buttermilk, then dredge in the flour mixture. Cook chicken pieces in oil 4 to 5 minutes, until they reach an internal temperature of 160°F, turning chicken over halfway through the cooking process. Drain on paper towels.

ASSEMBLE

Spread some Sriracha mayo on top half of brioche bun and aioli mayo on bottom half. Place fried chicken on bottom half of bun, topping with a hearty portion of cabbage slaw and top half of bun. Enjoy.

KOBE BURGERS WITH KING CRAB TEMPURA AND FOIE GRAS

BURGERS

2½ pounds Kobe beef (chuck, short rib and sirloin meat)
½ pound foie gras, finely minced
½ cup white miso paste

TEMPURA KING CRAB

¾ pound king crab legs, steamed, chilled, meat removed and cut into big chunks
Canola (or vegetable) oil, for frying
Tempura Batter:
¼ cup all-purpose flour
¼ cup rice flour
½ cup beer
½ teaspoon sea salt
½ cup all-purpose flour, for dredging

BLACK TRUFFLE SPREAD

2 tablespoons Mayonnaise (page 210)
3 tablespoons black truffle sauce
½ teaspoon black truffle oil
½ teaspoon balsamic glaze
½ teaspoon lemon juice

FOR ASSEMBLY

2 ounces microgreens
Scant ¼ teaspoon truffle oil
½ teaspoon freshly squeezed lemon juice
1 large (or 2 small) heirloom tomatoes, cut into ¼-inch-thick slices
4 (3½-4-inch) brioche buns

PREPARE BURGER MIX

Ask if your local butcher can grind the beef for you. If not, at home pass Kobe beef through grinder twice. Combine ground meat with foie gras and miso in a bowl, mixing well. Shape into 4 burger patties. Cover and set aside.

MAKE TEMPURA KING CRAB

Heat canola oil in a heavy-bottomed stockpot or frying pan to 375°F. Whisk together all ingredients for the tempura batter in a bowl, creating a smooth batter. Dredge crab pieces in flour, then dip into tempura batter. Fry for about 2 minutes, until golden brown. Drain crab on paper towels.

PREPARE BLACK TRUFFLE SPREAD

Combine all ingredients in a small bowl, making sure to mix well. Set aside.

ASSEMBLE

Preheat skillet and cook burgers to desired doneness over medium heat. While burgers are cooking, lightly toss microgreens in a bowl with truffle oil and lemon juice. Lay tomato slice and burger on bottom half of bun. Top with a generous portion of microgreen salad, a few pieces of tempura king crab and black truffle spread. Cap burger with top half of bun.

LOBSTER REUBEN

LOBSTER SALAD

1 (1½-pound) whole lobster, steamed, cooled, meat removed and cut into ½-inch chunks
½ celery stalk (about ¼ cup), minced
¼ cup olive oil Mayonnaise (page 210)
1 tablespoon fresh cilantro, chopped
1 tablespoon freshly squeezed lemon juice
½ teaspoon Worcestershire sauce
¼ teaspoon freshly ground black pepper
Sea salt, to taste

RUSSIAN DRESSING

1 cup olive oil Mayonnaise (page 210)
½ cup ketchup
1 tablespoon red wine vinegar
2 tablespoons finely chopped green bell pepper
2 tablespoons minced cornichon pickle
2 tablespoons diced red onion
½ teaspoon sea salt
⅛ teaspoon freshly ground black pepper
Tabasco sauce, to taste

FOR ASSEMBLY

8 slices rye bread
1 (8-ounce) jar sauerkraut, drained
4 slices Swiss cheese
3 tablespoons unsalted butter, room temperature

PREPARE LOBSTER SALAD

Combine all ingredients in a bowl, seasoning to taste. Cover with plastic wrap and chill until ready to assemble sandwiches.

PREPARE RUSSIAN DRESSING

Whisk together all ingredients in a medium bowl until well blended. Add a few drops of Tabasco and season to taste. Cover and set aside.

ASSEMBLE

Preheat griddle or oven to 400°F. For each sandwich, take 2 slices of bread, buttering 1 side of each; turn over. On unbuttered side of 1 slice, spread 1 tablespoon Russian dressing and top with 1 slice Swiss cheese and some sauerkraut. On other slice of bread, spread ¼ cup lobster salad. Place each sandwich half (open-faced-sandwich style) butter side down on heated griddle or baking tray. Cook until lobster salad is heated through and the cheese has melted. Place the 2 halves of each sandwich together, cut and enjoy.

PASTRIES AND DESSERTS

SWEET ENDINGS

Leave With a Smile

I like my guests to leave with a smile on their faces. Since we are all about sea salt, many of our desserts take advantage of that happy marriage of sweet and savory.

In the following pages, you will find one example of this that's extra close to my heart: hot chocolate with Murray River salt and caramel. I love that combination so much that I designed our signature dessert as an artistic tower of dark chocolate made with caramel and sea salt. It is so beautiful and delicious.

You will also see that some of my recipes call for unique flavors of sorbet and gelato, which we make in-house with fresh and organic ingredients. The gelato is very traditional with that nice, pudding-like mouthfeel. The green apple soufflé, for instance, I serve with a pistachio gelato—one of my favorite flavors. At Sea Salt and Barbatella, our more casual restaurant in Naples, we make many nice varieties such as mango, hazelnut, praline, mocha fudge and roasted coconut. Lighter than ice cream, the gelato is another way to end the meal on a sweet note that doesn't make you feel overloaded with richness.

Dessert does not have to be complicated. I like to surprise my guests with a bowl of cotton candy after dinner. Everyone loves that.

Some of the recipes in this chapter I created specially for this cookbook. They're original surprises to share with your family and friends that are guaranteed to bring your meal to a sweet ending of smiles.

GREEN APPLE SOUFFLÉ

A refreshing, warm dessert. It's difficult to describe with words; only your palate can appreciate it.

Serves 8

SOUFFLÉ BASE

1 Granny Smith apple, cored but not peeled
1 cup milk
⅓ cup superfine sugar, divided
1 egg
3 tablespoons plus 2 teaspoons cornstarch

SOUFFLÉ

5 tablespoons unsalted butter, melted
⅓ cup superfine sugar, plus more for dusting
1 teaspoon cornstarch
5 egg whites

ASSEMBLY

Powdered sugar
Pistachio Gelato (page 211)

PREPARE SOUFFLÉ BASE

Chop apple roughly and place in a food processor. Process to a very smooth purée. Push apple purée through a sieve with the back of a soup ladle to remove any fibrous bits. Set aside.

Combine milk and half the sugar in a saucepan and bring to a boil. In a separate bowl, beat egg with remaining sugar and cornstarch. Pour half the boiling milk over egg mixture and whisk well. Tip egg mixture back into the saucepan with remaining milk. Cook over medium heat, whisking constantly, for 2 minutes or until custard thickens. Stir in apple purée and bring back to a boil. Remove from heat, place in a bowl and cover with plastic wrap.

FINISH SOUFFLÉ

Preheat oven to 320°F. Using a pastry brush, grease the insides of 8 (6-ounce) soufflé dishes with melted butter. Brush in an upward direction only. Dust evenly with sugar, tapping out any excess. Set aside. Mix superfine sugar with cornstarch. Place egg whites in the bowl of an electric mixer and whisk at moderate speed to form soft peaks. Lower speed and sprinkle in the sugar-cornstarch mixture. Increase speed to high and whisk until evenly combined and the whites begin to become stiff and shiny, about 3 minutes. Place soufflé base in a large mixing bowl. Spoon half of the whipped egg whites on top and use a spatula to fold them in, gently and evenly. Repeat with remaining whites. Fill prepared soufflé dishes to the rim, using a spatula to level the surface. Arrange soufflé dishes on a cookie sheet and bake for 8 to 12 minutes, until well risen and lightly browned. Dust tops with powdered sugar. Serve immediately with gelato.

HOT CHOCOLATE, MURRAY RIVER SALT, CARAMEL

Hot chocolate was one of my favorite things to drink in wintertime on ski trips. So I thought, why not serve it as a liquid dessert? We finish it with Murray River salt and caramel—one of my favorite flavor combinations.

Serves 5

HOT CHOCOLATE

2 cups whole milk
½ cup heavy cream
¾ cup chopped milk chocolate couverture (65 percent cocoa butter)
3 tablespoons sugar
2 tablespoons plus 2 teaspoons extra-brute cocoa powder

FOR ASSEMBLY

Murray River sea salt
Caramel Sauce (page 208)
Whipped cream

PREPARE HOT CHOCOLATE

Bring whole milk to a boil in a small saucepot. Place heavy cream in a medium bowl. Remove milk from heat and add to the bowl. Add chocolate, sugar and cocoa powder. Stir until chocolate has melted. Refrigerate for 12 hours.

ASSEMBLE

Reheat hot chocolate to 140°F. Pour into pasta bowls and top with whipped cream. Drizzle caramel over whipped cream and sprinkle sea salt on top.

STRAWBERRY AND BALSAMIC MASCARPONE GELATO WITH PINK PEPPERCORNS AND MINT

We have served this dessert for a long time, even back at our Washington, D.C., restaurants. Everyone loves it because it is unique without being difficult to prepare. All the different flavors come together and just melt on your tongue—it's a nice surprise.

Serves 6

MASCARPONE GELATO

1½ cups whole milk
¼ cup heavy cream
12 egg yolks
1 cup sugar
1½ cups mascarpone cheese
1 teaspoon lemon juice
2 tablespoons Grand Marnier

STRAWBERRIES

5 cups strawberries
½ cup sugar
⅓ cup balsamic vinegar

FOR ASSEMBLY

12 leaves mint
1 tablespoon pink peppercorns

PREPARE MASCARPONE GELATO

Heat milk and cream in a pot to 190°F. Whisk egg yolks and sugar in a large bowl. Temper cream mixture by whisking a little at a time into yolks. After 2 ladlefuls, combine completely. Whisk in mascarpone, lemon juice and Grand Marnier, mixing until completely uniform. Strain into an ice-cream maker and process according to manufacturer's directions. Freeze gelato until ready to plate.

PREPARE STRAWBERRIES

Rinse and quarter strawberries. Mix sugar and balsamic vinegar with strawberries in a large bowl. Let sit for 5 minutes.

ASSEMBLE

Divide strawberries among 6 bowls. Top with a scoop of mascarpone gelato. Garnish with mint and pink peppercorns.

LEMON SORBET WITH MANGO-FENNEL SALSA

When I was a boy, we would cut a lemon in half, stick a piece of licorice in it, then lick the licorice and the lemon. This recipe, while more elegant, brings a smile to my face because it reminds me of that memory. It was the most simple thing to enjoy, even with only a few cents in my pocket.

Serves 6

LEMON SORBET
1 cup water
1 cup sugar
1 egg white
1 cup lemon juice
2 tablespoons glucose

CANDIED FENNEL
⅓ cup black sambuca
1 cup fennel, diced
3 peels lemon zest
⅓ cup soft black licorice, chopped
1 cup water

MANGO SALSA
½ cup mango, diced

FOR ASSEMBLY
2 sprigs dill, stems removed

PREPARE LEMON SORBET

Bring water and sugar to a boil in a small saucepot. Remove from heat and chill. Mix egg white and lemon juice together in a bowl. Whisk in glucose. Process in an ice-cream maker according to manufacturer's directions. Freeze sorbet until ready to plate.

PREPARE CANDIED FENNEL

Combine all ingredients in a small saucepot. Bring to a boil, then lower heat and simmer for 5 to 7 minutes. Remove from heat and remove lemon zest. Let cool.

PREPARE MANGO SALSA

Mix candied fennel and mango together.

ASSEMBLE

Scoop lemon sorbet into each bowl. Top with salsa and dill.

ROASTED PEAR SOUP WITH AMARONE-BLACK PEPPER SORBET

Sbrisolona is a cross between a biscotti and a scone. It has a crumbly texture so you can deconstruct it for a nice effect in this dish. Amarone is one of the richest wines in the world. It's made with dry grapes and perfect for this gelato. You'll be surprised what a sprinkle of ground pepper adds to it. Someone recently told me it tastes like jelly on toast.

Serves 8

GELATO

1 cup milk
1 cup heavy cream
2 peels orange zest
½ teaspoon coarsely ground black pepper
½ cup sugar
7 egg yolks
1½ cups Amarone wine
¼ cup Raspberry Juice (page 208)

SBRISOLONA

2¼ cups 00 flour
½ cup plus 2 tablespoons cornmeal
1 cup plus 1½ tablespoons sugar
1 tablespoon baking powder
Zest of ½ lemon
¾ pounds butter
4 egg yolks
3 tablespoons almonds, unpeeled

PEAR SOUP

9 Roasted Pears (page 212)
¾ cup braising liquid from the pears, strained and chilled
¾ cup Raspberry Juice (page 208)
¾ cup water

PREPARE GELATO

Heat milk, cream, zest and pepper in a saucepot over medium heat until simmering. Whisk sugar and egg yolks together in a large bowl. Slowly pour half the hot milk mixture into the eggs, whisking constantly. Add egg yolk mixture to pot and cook, stirring constantly, for a few minutes. Whisk in wine and raspberry juice. Strain into an ice-cream maker and process according to manufacturer's directions. Freeze until ready to plate.

PREPARE SBRISOLONA

Preheat oven to 350°F. Line a 9-inch springform pan with parchment paper and baking spray. Whisk together flour, cornmeal, sugar, baking powder and lemon zest in a large bowl. Cut in butter using a pastry blender until mixture resembles a coarse meal. Add egg yolks and work in gently with your hands, being careful not to overmix; the dough should be crumbly and look like crumble topping. Pour crumbs into the prepared pan and gently press crumbs around the edges and lightly across the top. The surface should be uneven and dimpled. Scatter almonds on top and gently press them into the dough. Bake for 40 minutes or until a deep golden brown. Transfer to a rack and let cool completely before unmolding.

PREPARE PEAR SOUP

Combine roasted pears, braising liquid, raspberry juice and water in a large bowl.

Puree in batches in a blender on high speed for 1 minute until smooth.

ASSEMBLE

Divide soup among 8 bowls. Place a scoop of gelato in the center of each bowl. Crumble sbrisolona over top of soup.

MENTA GELATO WITH THREE-CHOCOLATE BRITTLE

Menta liqueur is used as a digestif. It has a nice, strong, herbal flavor. We love it mixed with chocolate as a cocktail. This gelato dish takes those flavors out from the glass for a beautiful dessert.

CHOCOLATE BRITTLE

¾ cup dark chocolate (at least 60 percent cocoa), finely chopped
¾ cup milk chocolate, finely chopped
¾ cup white chocolate, finely chopped
2 quarts liquid nitrogen

MENTA GELATO

2 cups (1 pint) heavy cream
2 quarts (½ gallon) whole milk
3 vanilla beans, split and scraped
15 egg yolks
2 cups (14 ounces) sugar
½ cup mint paste
2 tablespoons mint syrup
½ cup Fernet Branca Menta

PREPARE BRITTLE

Melt each chocolate separately over low heat in a double boiler, stirring frequently. Be sure water never heats above a simmer. Set each one aside.

In a heavy-duty stainless-steel stockpot, pour liquid nitrogen to a depth of about ⅔-inch. Slowly trickle in 1 type of melted chocolate at a time, continuously mixing with liquid nitrogen using a long-handle stainless-steel spoon. Once set, remove chocolate with slotted spoon or spider. Set aside to cool before serving.

PREPARE GELATO

Place cream, milk and vanilla bean pulp in a heavy-bottomed stockpot over medium heat. Cook, stirring occasionally, until just before boiling or when it reaches about 195°F. Remove from heat and reserve in pot.

In a large mixing bowl, combine yolks with sugar, whisking together until thick and creamy. Add heated milk mixture one ladle at a time, beating vigorously with a whisk. Continue just until yolk mixture feels warm. Pour warmed yolk mixture slowly into remaining milk mixture, beating with whisk. Add mint paste, mint syrup and Fernet Branca Menta, mixing well. Pour combined mixture into a bowl and refrigerate. Process in a gelato maker according to manufacturer's directions.

To serve, either fold brittle into gelato or sprinkle on top as a garnish.

**Note: Dry ice is extremely cold and can cause frostbite. Always use leather gloves or a kitchen towel when handling dry ice.*

DATE CRÈME BRÛLÉE WITH KAHLÚA

Crème brûlée lovers will savor this creation, a delicious evolution of a classic dessert.

Serves 10

CUSTARD
5 cups heavy cream
10 egg yolks
¼ cup plus 1 tablespoon superfine sugar
1 vanilla bean, split and seeds scraped
1 cinnamon stick

DATE CONFIT
½ cup plus 2 tablespoons superfine sugar
½ cup water
8 ounces fresh whole dates
½ cup Kahlúa

FOR ASSEMBLY
½ cup superfine sugar

PREPARE CUSTARD

Bring cream to a rolling boil over medium-high heat in a large heavy-bottomed saucepot. In a large bowl, whisk together egg yolks, sugar, vanilla bean and its scrapings, and cinnamon stick. Pour hot cream onto the yolk mixture and whisk well. Pour mixture back into the pot and reduce heat to medium. Cook gently for 15 to 20 minutes, stirring constantly with a wooden spoon, until custard thickens. It should be as thick as honey and just beginning to catch on the bottom of the pot. Strain mixture into a stainless-steel or glass bowl and sit it in an ice bath for 5 to 10 minutes. This is an important step as it stops the custard from cooking further. Remove from ice and allow to continue cooling at room temperature.

PREPARE DATE CONFIT

Heat sugar with water in a heavy-bottomed saucepot over medium-high heat until completely dissolved. Add dates and Kahlúa and cover liquid's surface with a circle of parchment paper to keep the dates submerged and prevent a skin from forming during cooking. Reduce heat to low and gently cook for 15 to 20 minutes, until golden brown. Remove from heat and let cool to the touch. Remove pits and skins from dates and chop them fine.

ASSEMBLE

Place 1 heaping teaspoon confit at the bottom of 10 small glasses or ramekins. Spoon enough custard into dishes to fill to just below the rim, then refrigerate. When ready to serve, lightly dust custards with sugar. Use a domestic blowtorch to caramelize the sugar, then return to fridge for 5 minutes. Dust with a little more sugar and repeat. This ensures a good, even layer of crunchy toffee. If you are using heatproof glasses, you could alternatively grill the brûlées under a very hot broiler until sugar is brown and bubbling.

WATERMELON, BERRY, PISTACHIO HALVA SALAD

This is a great dessert when you wish to finish a meal with something refreshing and healthy.

Serves 4

PISTACHIO HALVA

1¼ cups pistachios, shelled
2 tablespoons milk
½ cup sugar
1½ tablespoons butter or ghee
1 tablespoon vanilla extract

VANILLA SUGAR SYRUP

¼ cup superfine sugar
3 tablespoons plus 1 teaspoon water
½ vanilla bean, split, seeds scraped
Zest of ½ lemon

FOR ASSEMBLY

1 seedless watermelon, small (about 1 pound)
8 ounces blackberries
8 ounces raspberries
8 ounces strawberries
⅓ cup mint leaves, finely shredded
Elderflower sprigs (optional)
3½ ounces Pistachio Halva (above), crumbled

PREPARE PISTACHIO HALVA

Place pistachios in a bowl, top with boiling water and soak for 30 minutes. Grease and line an 8 x 8-inch square pan with wax paper. Drain pistachios thoroughly and place in a blender or food processor. Add milk and process until finely chopped. Scrape mixture down from sides of the blender once or twice during the process. Stir in sugar. Place a large nonstick skillet over medium-low heat and melt butter until it starts to bubble. Add nut paste and cook for about 15 minutes, stirring constantly, until mixture is very thick. Stir in vanilla extract. Spoon mixture into the prepared pan and spread evenly. Let cool completely. Cut into 20 squares using a sharp knife.

PREPARE VANILLA SUGAR SYRUP

Place all ingredients in a small saucepan. Bring to a boil over medium-high heat, then simmer gently for about 5 minutes. Remove from heat. When cool, remove vanilla bean (this can be washed and reused to flavor your canister of sugar). Chill syrup until ready to use.

ASSEMBLE

Use a melon baller to scoop out balls of watermelon. Place in a mixing bowl with berries, mint and elderflower, if using, and pour chilled syrup over fruit. Gently stir, then remove sprigs and divide among 4 serving bowls. Top with crumbled halva and serve immediately.

COCKTAILS

LIQUID WORKS OF ART

Potable Passion

‡

My director of wine and spirits, Liset Zelaya, is very creative when it comes to inventing new cocktails with fresh ingredients. I encourage her to use fresh herbs in her recipes as much as possible. Everything needs to be high quality—period. We even give our customers the choice of premium mixers, such as a brand of Indian tonic water. It makes such a difference when paired with Hendrick's in a gin and tonic, which is one of my favorite summer drinks.

A good cocktail is so much more than a few ingredients poured together. It's like any work of art. A good cocktail must have character. It must be properly executed. For example, my bartenders know I love my martinis shaken so thoroughly that there's almost a sheen of ice at the top of the glass. There's the art!

Some of the touches that make our cocktails artful are our use of small-batch craft spirits, fresh seasonal ingredients, our own barrel-aged bourbons and house-infused vodkas.

We always have freshly squeezed orange, lime and lemon juices in the bar refrigerator year-round. But then in the summer, Liset invents pineapple mojitos, coconut water cocktails, blood orange refreshers and watermelon martinis. The fall and winter months bring on spiced pear martinis, apple cinnamon tequila and blueberry and rosemary bourbon cocktails.

We like to infuse our cocktails with a variety of fresh greens, fruits and herbs, including celery and parsley, peaches and many different berries, lemongrass and ginger—all have found their way into our refreshingly original infusions. And don't be surprised to find our bartenders muddling rosemary into our cocktails—we're always looking for new ways to bring something inventive and fun to our guests.

The fact that our bar is open to the outdoors dictates, in some ways, how we design our drinks. It creates such a perfect Naples atmosphere of conviviality and fine libations. You can just taste the love and passion.

SEA SALT BLOODY MARY

INFUSED VODKA

Makes 1 quart

3 stalks celery
½ bell pepper, cut into 1-inch strips
1 large onion, quartered
1 jalapeño pepper, halved (remove seeds and membranes for less heat)
4 stems fresh cilantro
4 stems fresh parsley
4 stems fresh basil
1 tablespoon peeled and coarsely chopped fresh ginger
1 quart vodka

BLOODY MARY MIX

Makes 1 quart

1 quart tomato juice (fresh tomato juice recommended)
½ teaspoon celery seed powder
3 tablespoons fresh horseradish, grated
1 tablespoon salt
½ teaspoon black pepper
½ teaspoon white pepper
2 drops Tabasco
2 drops Worcestershire sauce
Juice of 3 lemons

BLOODY MARY COCKTAIL

Serves 1

Smoked habanero salt
Ice
2 ounces Infused Vodka
Pickled vegetables of choice

MAKE INFUSED VODKA

Cut celery stalks to height of 1-quart jar.Place in jar with remaining ingredients, adding vodka until full. Let sit at room temperature for 7 to 10 days. Do not wait more than 10 days to remove all vegetables and herbs. Strain through cheesecloth.

MAKE BLOODY MARY MIX

Combine all ingredients in a pitcher and stir well. Store unused mix in an airtight container in the refrigerator for up to 2 weeks. (If you cannot

   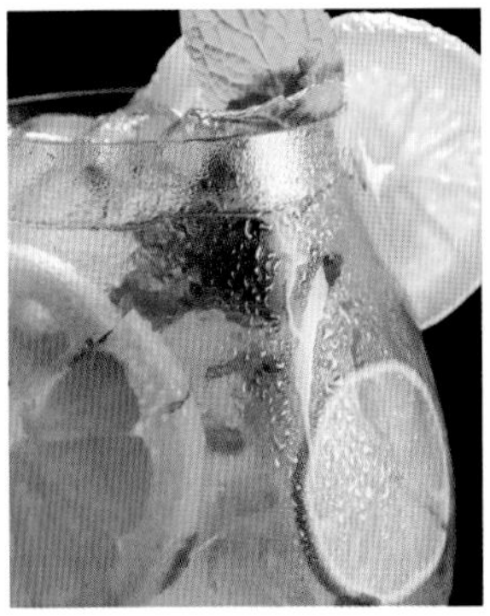

find celery seed powder, grind celery seed with mortar and pestle.)

ASSEMBLE

Rim glass with salt and fill with ice. Pour vodka and add Bloody Mary mix to taste. Stir well, then garnish with pickled vegetables.

BLUEBERRY BULLEIT

Makes 1 cocktail

½ teaspoon wild blueberry preserves
2 ounces Bulleit Bourbon
½ ounce Pama Pomegranate Liqueur
Juice of ¼ lemon
Ice
Ginger ale
1 sprig fresh rosemary
3 fresh or frozen blueberries

Place preserves in rocks glass. Add bourbon, liqueur and lemon juice. Stir. Fill glass with ice and then briskly stir again. Top with a splash of ginger ale and garnish with rosemary and blueberries.

ITALIAN SUMMER

Makes 1 cocktail

1 large strawberry, halved
2 leaves basil
3 drops balsamic vinegar
2 ounces Hangar 1 vodka
½ ounce St. Germain Elderflower Liqueur
Ice
1½ ounces soda
Strawberry, for garnish

In a tall glass, muddle strawberry, basil and balsamic vinegar. Mix in vodka and St. Germain. Add ice and top with soda, then garnish.

LOLA CHERRY COLA

Makes 1 cocktail

This is our homage to the Cuba libre beverage and the famous song by the Kinks.

CHERRY-INFUSED RUM

750-milliliter bottle Ron Matusalem Gran Reserva rum
4 ounces maraschino cherries, stemmed
2 ounces sweet vermouth

FOR ASSEMBLY

Ice
2½ ounces Cherry-Infused Rum
2–3 ounces Coca-Cola
1 rum-soaked cherry

MAKE INFUSED RUM

In a container with lid and at least 32-ounce capacity, place cherries and sweet vermouth. Add entire contents of rum bottle, cover and let sit for at least 1 week. Reserve cherries.

ASSEMBLE

Fill rocks glass with ice. Add rum, top with soda and garnish with cherry.

MANDARINE MOJITO

Makes 1 cocktail

2 lime quarters
6 mint leaves, ripped to release aroma
2 ounces Wicked Dolphin silver rum
¼ ounce Mandarine Napoléon
Splash of agave nectar
Ice, for shaking and serving
Soda
Lime and orange slices, for garnish

In a cocktail shaker, gently muddle limes and mint leaves. Add remaining ingredients and shake vigorously. Pour over ice in a tall glass. Top with a splash of soda, then add garnish.

NAPLES NEGRONI

Makes 1 cocktail

Ice
1 ounce Campari
1 ounce Nolet's gin
1 ounce Dolin Vermouth Rouge
1 ounce Prosecco

Over ice in a rocks glass, add Campari, gin and vermouth. Stir. Top with Prosecco.

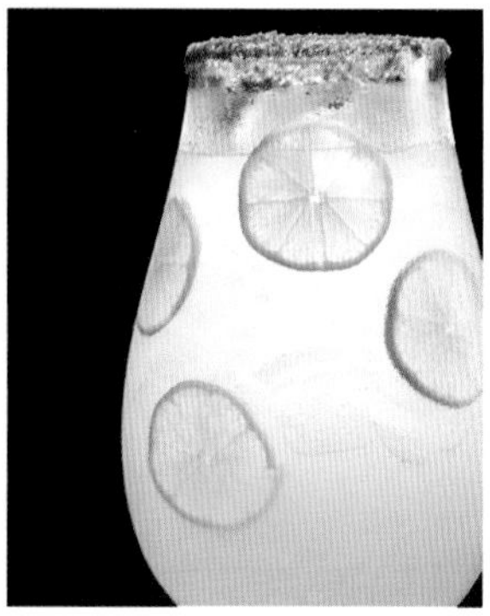
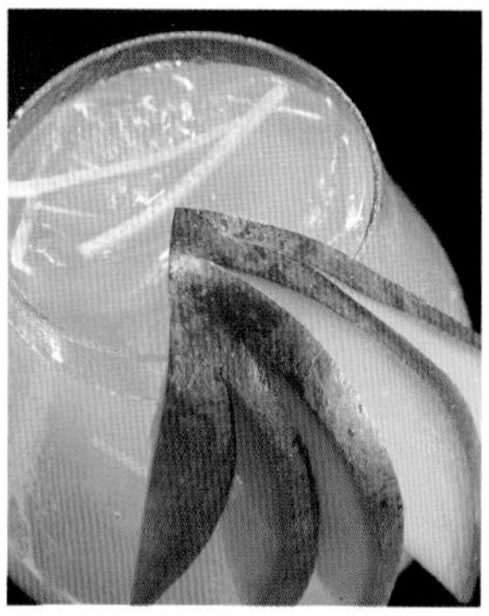

PEACH KISS

You can substitute a commercial peach-infused rum in this cocktail, but if you have the time then it's much better and tastier to make your own.

PEACH-INFUSED RUM

750-milliliter bottle white rum
4 ripe peaches, 2 reserved

FOR ASSEMBLY

2 ounces Peach-Infused Rum
¼ ounce Domaine de Canton ginger liqueur
Ice
¼ ounce brut rosé champagne
Peach slice, for garnish

MAKE INFUSED RUM (7 DAYS AHEAD)

Quarter 2 peaches. In a wide-mouth jar with lid, combine slices with rum. Cover and let sit. After 4 days, quarter remaining peaches. Remove original and replace with the new peaches. Infusion is complete after 1 week.

ASSEMBLE

In a shaker, mix rum and ginger liqueur. Add ice and shake vigorously. Pour into a martini glass. Top with champagne to give the cocktail a soft peach hue and effervescence. Garnish with a floating peach slice.

SEA SALT MARGARITA

Makes 1 cocktail

2 ounces Casamigos reposado, or other premium tequila
¼ ounce Mandarine Napoléon
Juice of 1 lime
¼ ounce agave nectar
Ice

FOR ASSEMBLY

Alaea red clay salt, or other sea salt
1 lime slice

Shake all ingredients with ice. Rim glass with salt, pour in cocktail and garnish with lime.

SEA SALT SIDECAR

Makes 1 cocktail

1 fresh mango, puréed
2 ounces Camus Cognac VS
½ ounce Mandarine Napoléon
Juice of ¼ lemon
Soda
Lemon and mango slices, for garnish

Slice mango and place in a blender. Pulse until puréed, then strain through a chinois to remove pulp.

In a shaker, combine ½ ounce mango purée with cognacs and lemon juice. Shake and pour into a rocks glass. Top with a splash of soda and garnish with lemon and mango.

SEASIDE LEMONADE

Makes 1 cocktail

3 ripe raspberries
2½ ounces Nolet's gin
Crushed ice
2 ounces freshly squeezed lemonade
Fresh raspberry and lemon slice, for garnish

In a tall glass, crush raspberries and muddle with gin. Fill glass with crushed ice and top with lemonade. Garnish with raspberry and lemon.

WINE & DINE

Stories in a Bottle

Our wine room is bulging with wines. But that's not even the half of it. We also have a storage location where we age some of our more robust red wines, including lots of big Italians.

I would be lying if I were to say I'm not partial to Italian wine. As with food, I am passionate about wine, and I only want the best. And what's good about Italian wines is that their grapes grow in the very same regions where their delicious food counterparts also come from. The vintners in those areas specifically make wines to complement regional products.

We carry 50 varieties of Italian wines alone, but despite my bias toward Italian wine, we also carry hundreds of others. We have more than 5,000 bottles from all over the world in inventory, carefully curated by our sommelier Liset Zelaya, a certified specialist of wine through the Society of Wine Educators and certified sommelier through the Master Court of Sommeliers. She and I team together to vet the finest wines and create what I believe is one of the most carefully, beautifully designed wine lists around.

Liset finds my favorite wines, no matter how rare. She told me that finding my all-time love, Tenuta dell'Ornallaia, Messeto, was like looking for a "needle in a haystack." It's a beautiful merlot that's a very specific, select vintage. But she succeeded, and I have to admit that every time I see her serving it to a customer, I get a little jealous. It is so wonderful to drink—it makes me feel so good and relaxed. I get goosebumps just thinking about it.

Ingrid and I travel every summer to spend time with our vintners and taste new wines and food products. Liset does also, then we all bring back the vintners' stories to share with our customers. They love that. It gives the wine a lovely sense of place that they, too, will remember whenever they drink it again.

The three of us also plan amazing vintner dinners. At one, our guests dined and wined while they watched a midnight harvest of grapes in Italy by podcast. Guests gain a new appreciation for wine when they see things like that. We work hard at taking the intimidation out of wine by helping our customers select from our vast, 25-page menu.

Liset and I have a lot of fun making the perfect marriage of food and wine—one of the most beautiful marriages in the world. We showcase this at my Chef's Table dinners, where we work to make the two complement one another. If Liset has decided to pour a certain wine, she tells me its characteristics, and I make adjustments in seasoning and flavors in my food.

At Barbatella, we have an Enomatic machine, which dispenses 32 different kinds of wine by the glass without fear of them losing their peak flavor. At Sea Salt, we change the wine menu every day. We pour nearly 30 wines by the glass and offer three wine flights. We've even discovered a new device called a Coravin that allows us to replicate what the Enomatic does but on a smaller scale, so you can have a taste of an expensive wine without uncorking and investing in the whole bottle.

This wonderful combination of good food and good wine doesn't have to be expensive. Our menu includes some top-end wines, but also some very affordable wines.

Food and wine are like fashion trends. People's tastes are fickle, so chefs and vintners must forever change what they are creating. That's why it is important to have people like us who are passionate about wine and can let you know what's new and worthy of your palate.

PANTRY

BEEF JUS

Makes 1 quart

20 pounds beef knuckle bones, cut into 2-inch pieces
5 pounds beef short ribs
3 pounds veal feet
¼ cup grapeseed oil
2 cups sliced button mushrooms
4 cups sliced onions
2 cups diced carrots
2 cups diced celery
2 cups diced celery root
2 cups sliced leeks
½ cup tomato paste
4 cups red wine
10 sprigs thyme
25 black peppercorns
2 bay leaves
30 pounds ice cubes, plus more for chilling

Preheat oven to 375°F. Spread beef bones, short ribs and veal feet in a single layer on 2 large cookie sheets. Roast until golden brown, 45 minutes to 1 hour, turning the bones and feet after 30 minutes.

Meanwhile, place oil in a 20-quart stockpot over high heat. Sauté mushrooms, onions, carrots, celery, celery root and leeks until caramelized, 10 to 15 minutes. Add tomato paste and sauté until caramelized, 5 to 7 minutes. Add wine and reduce to the consistency of syrup.

Add roasted meat and the thyme, peppercorns and bay leaves and cover with 30 pounds ice. Bring to a simmer over medium heat and skim the stock of all impurities and fats that rise to the top. Reduce heat to low and continue to simmer, uncovered, for 5 hours, skimming every 30 minutes. Strain through a chinois, then return to heat and reduce to 1 quart. Strain again and chill over remaining ice.

BEEF STOCK

Makes 1 gallon

5 pounds beef bones
2 pounds beef breast, cut into 2-inch pieces
3 pounds veal feet, cut into 2-inch pieces
20 pounds ice cubes, plus more for chilling
1 cup sliced onion
½ cup diced carrots
½ cup diced celery
½ cup diced celery root
½ cup diced leeks, white parts only
½ cup sliced button mushrooms
2 cups white wine
10 white peppercorns
5 sprigs thyme
1 bay leaf

Rinse bones well under running water for 5 minutes. Place bones, beef breast and veal feet in a 20-quart stockpot. Cover with ice and bring to a simmer over medium heat. Skim impurities and fats off top, then add remaining ingredients. Simmer, uncovered, for 4 hours, skimming every 30 minutes. Strain stock through cheesecloth and chill over ice.

BERRY JUICE

1 cup fresh strawberries or raspberries
2 teaspoons lemon juice
1 tablespoon sugar
¼ cup cold water

Wash berries and drain. If using strawberries, stem and cut them into pieces. Add all ingredients to a blender and puree until smooth. Store in refrigerator for up to 1 week.

MEAT AND POULTRY BRINE

1 cup sea salt
1 cup brown sugar
2 tablespoons juniper berries
1 teaspoon whole black peppercorns
2 heads garlic, halved crosswise
4 (5-inch) sprigs fresh thyme
Zest of 6 lemons
6 bay leaves
4 cups water
10 cups ice cubes

Excluding the ice, combine all ingredients in a pot. Bring to a boil, then lower heat and simmer for 5 minutes. Remove from heat and add ice to cool.

TO USE BRINE

Place meat or poultry in a container and cover with brine. Cover container and brine according to recipe directions.

CARAMEL SAUCE

Makes 1 cup

1 cup sugar
¼ cup water
¾ cup heavy cream
3½ tablespoons unsalted butter

Combine the sugar and water in a heavy-bottomed saucepot over medium-low heat until the sugar dissolves. Increase the heat and bring to a boil, without stirring. Boil until the syrup is a deep amber color, about 5 to 6 minutes. Remove the sugar from the heat and carefully whisk in the heavy cream. The mixture will bubble and be very hot. Be careful not to touch at this stage. Stir in the butter and transfer the caramel to a dish to cool.

CHICKEN STOCK

Makes 1 gallon

10 pounds chicken backs and necks
15 pounds ice cubes, plus more for chilling
1 cup diced leeks, white parts only
½ cup chopped celery
½ cup chopped celery root
½ cup sliced shallots
½ cup chopped fennel, bulb only
½ cup sliced white onion
5 white peppercorns
1 bay leaf
1 (6-inch) sprig thyme

Rinse chicken parts well under running water for 5 minutes. Place in a 20-quart stockpot, top with ice, cover and bring to a simmer over medium heat. Skim foam and fats off top, then add remaining ingredients. Simmer, uncovered, for 3 hours, skimming and then stirring every 30 minutes. Strain stock through cheesecloth and chill over ice. Refrigerate stock until fat cap hardens, 6 to 8 hours. Remove fat and discard. Store in refrigerator for up to 1 week, or freeze by cupfuls in small bags or containers for future use.

CRÈME FRAÎCHE

1 cup whipping cream
2 tablespoons buttermilk

Combine cream and buttermilk in a saucepan and heat only until tepid, no more than 85°F.

Pour into a clean glass jar. Partially cover and let stand at room temperature (between 65°F and 75°F) for 8 to 24 hours or until thick. Stir, and refrigerate for at least 24 hours before using. It will keep for about 2 weeks in the refrigerator.

DUCK JUS

Makes 4 cups

10 pounds duck carcasses, cut into 2-inch pieces
3 pounds chicken feet
4 tablespoons duck fat
4 cups onions, sliced
2 cups carrots, diced
2 cups celery, diced
2 cups celery root, diced
2 cups leeks, diced
5 tablespoons tomato paste
2 cups port
½ cup cognac
3 cups red wine
10 sprigs thyme
2 bay leaves
5 juniper berries
25 peppercorns
2 gallons Chicken Stock (page 209)

Pre-heat the oven to 375°F. Line 2 large rimmed baking sheets with aluminum foil. Spread the duck bones and chicken feet in a single layer on the baking sheets and roast the bones in the oven until golden brown, approximately 1 hour and 15 minutes to 1 hour and 30 minutes, turning the bones over once after 20 minutes. Melt the duck fat in a 20-quart stockpot over high heat. Sauté the onions, carrots, celery, celery root and leeks in the duck fat until they caramelize, about 7 to 10 minutes. Add the tomato paste and sauté until caramelized, 5 to 7 minutes. Add the port and cognac and reduce by half. Add the red wine, thyme, bay leaves, juniper berries and peppercorns and reduce to syrup consistency. Add the chicken feet and carcass bones to the stockpot and cover with the chicken stock. Bring to a simmer over medium heat and skim the stock of all impurities and fats that rise to the top. Simmer, uncovered, over low heat for 5 hours, skimming every 30 minutes. Strain through a fine-mesh chinois and reduce to 1 quart. Strain again and chill over ice.

DUCK WING STOCK

Makes 2 quarts

5 pounds duck wings
2 pounds duck or chicken feet
1 cup diced leeks, white parts only
½ cup diced celery
½ cup diced celery root
½ cup sliced shallots
½ cup diced fennel
½ cup sliced white onion
5 white peppercorns
1 bay leaf
1 sprig thyme
4 cloves garlic
1 tablespoon juniper berries

Place duck wings and feet in a 10-quart stockpot, covering with water 1 to 2 inches above the bones. Bring to a simmer over medium heat. Skim impurities and fats off top, then add remaining ingredients. Simmer, uncovered, for 3 hours, skimming every 30 minutes. Strain stock through cheesecloth and chill.

FISH FUMET

Makes 1 gallon

5 tablespoons grapeseed oil
2 cups diced leeks, white parts only
2 cups sliced button mushrooms
1 cup diced celery
1 cup diced celery root
1 cup sliced shallots
1 cup diced fennel
4 cups white wine
1 lemon, cut in half
10 white peppercorns
3 bay leaves
12 pounds white-fish bones, heads included, no gills, cut into 2-inch pieces, cleaned of all blood and thoroughly rinsed
10 pounds ice cubes

Heat oil in a 20-quart stockpot over medium heat. Sweat all vegetables for 10 minutes. Add wine, lemon, peppercorns and bay leaves and reduce for 3 to 5 minutes. Add fish bones and 7 pounds of ice. Bring to a simmer over medium heat and skim away any impurities or fats that rise to the surface. Simmer gently for 30 minutes; do not allow to boil. Remove from heat and let rest for 10 minutes. Skim again and ladle the fumet out, straining through cheesecloth. Do not touch the fish bones, keeping the stock clear. Chill fumet over remaining ice.

LAMB JUS

Makes 1 quart

Ingredients
15 pounds lamb neck bones
¼ cup grapeseed oil
2 cups sliced button mushrooms
4 cups onions, sliced
2 cups carrots, diced
2 cups celery, diced
2 cups celery root, diced
2 cups leeks, diced
½ cup tomato paste
4 cups red wine
10 sprigs thyme
5 bay leaves
25 black peppercorns
30 pounds ice cubes

Pre-heat the oven to 375°F. Spread the neck bones in a single layer on 2 large rimmed baking sheets and roast in the oven until golden brown, 1 hour and 15 to 1 hour and 30 minutes, turning every 30 minutes. Heat the oil in a 20-quart stockpot over high heat. Sauté the onions, carrots, celery, leeks and celery root until they caramelized, 10 to 15 minutes. Add the tomato paste and sauté until caramelize, 5 to 7 minutes. Add the red wine and reduce to a syrup consistency. Add thyme, bay leaves, peppercorns, neck bones to the stockpot and cover with the ice. Bring to a simmer over medium heat and skim off all of the impurities and fats that rise to the top. Simmer over low heat, uncovered, for 5 hours, skimming every 30 minutes. Strain through a fine-mesh chinois and reduce to 1 quart. Strain again and chill over the ice.

LOBSTER STOCK

Makes 1 gallon

10 pounds whole lobster (about 1½ pounds each)
½ cup grapeseed oil
2 cups sliced onions
1 cup roughly cut carrots
1 cup diced celery
1 cup diced leeks
1 cup diced fennel
4 cloves garlic
1 cup tomato paste
½ cup cognac
2 cups white wine
15 pounds ice cubes, plus more for chilling
5 sprigs thyme
5 sprigs tarragon
5 sprigs lemon verbena
20 white peppercorns

Cut each lobster in half and smash halves, shell on, then cut into quarters. Place oil in a 20-quart stockpot over high heat. Sauté the lobster parts (shells on) until browned on all sides, 10 to 12 minutes. Add onions, carrots, celery, leeks, fennel and garlic and sauté for 5 to 7 minutes, until tender. Add tomato paste and sauté for 4 to 5 minutes. Add cognac and reduce by three-quarters. Add white wine and reduce by three-quarters. Add remaining ingredients and bring to a simmer over medium heat. Skim off any impurities or fats that rise to the top. Simmer for 30 minutes and strain through a fine-mesh chinois. Return stock to stockpot, simmer and reduce to 1 gallon. Strain again, and chill over ice.

MAYONNAISE

Makes more than 1 cup

1 egg yolk
2 teaspoons lemon juice
1 cup grapeseed or olive oil
½ teaspoon salt

Whisk egg yolk and lemon juice together. Add oil a drop at a time, whisking briskly, until it begins to emulsify, then slowly pour in a thin stream. Whisk in salt. Refrigerate. Best when used within 3 to 5 days, but will keep longer.

ORANGE NECTAR

Makes about 2 cups

2 quarts freshly squeezed orange juice
½ cup grapeseed oil
1 tablespoon extra-virgin olive oil
Pinch of sea salt

Strain orange juice through a fine-mesh sieve to remove pulp. In a wide saucepan, reduce juice to a consistency that would coat the back of a spoon. Remove from heat and whisk in oils and salt.

PASTA DOUGH

1 cup semolina, plus more for dusting
7 egg yolks
1 pound 00 flour
1 tablespoon olive oil
¼ teaspoon salt
1 tablespoon butter (add only for filling pasta, to make it more stretchy)

Thoroughly sift together 1 cup 00 flour, semolina flour and salt. On a clean surface, make a mountain out of flour mixture, then make a deep well in center. Break egg yolks into the well and add olive oil. Whisk yolks very gently with a fork, gradually incorporating flour from the sides of the well. When mixture becomes too thick to mix with a fork, begin kneading with your hands.

Knead dough for 8 to 12 minutes, until smooth and supple. Dust dough and work surface with semolina as needed to keep dough from becoming sticky.

Wrap dough tightly in plastic wrap (or

leave dough in bowl and wrap bowl) and let rest at room temperature for 30 minutes.

PEA PURÉE

Makes 2 cups

2¼ cups shelled English peas (about 11 ounces; may substitute frozen green peas)
1½ quarts water, salted
Ice cubes
1 teaspoon sea salt

Place water in a pot and bring to a boil. Meanwhile, prepare an ice bath. Add peas to hot water and cook until very tender, 3 to 4 minutes. (If using frozen peas, follow cooking directions on package.) Using a slotted spoon, transfer peas to ice bath. Once chilled, drain peas and shake off excess water. Purée peas in a blender, adding ice cubes throughout the process to keep the purée cold. Purée until all peas are mashed. Push the purée through a fine-mesh tamis or sieve. Season with salt. Keep refrigerated.

PICKLED CELERY

1 cup water
2 tablespoons pickling spice mix
2 tablespoons white wine vinegar
2 tablespoons sugar
3 stalks celery, cut into batons 3 inches long, ¼ inch wide

In a small saucepot, bring water, spices, vinegar and sugar to a boil. Lower heat to medium and simmer for 2 minutes. Remove from heat, strain through a fine-mesh sieve and let cool in refrigerator. Add celery batons and refrigerate overnight, 8 to 12 hours.

PICKLED RED ONIONS

1 cup water
2 tablespoons pickling spice mix
2 tablespoons white wine vinegar
2 tablespoons sugar
1 medium red onion, julienned

In a small saucepot, bring water, spices, vinegar and sugar to a boil. Lower heat to medium and simmer for 2 minutes. Remove from heat, strain through a fine-mesh sieve and let cool in refrigerator. Add red onion and refrigerate overnight, 8 to 12 hours.

PISTACHIO GELATO

15 egg yolks
2 cups (1 pint) heavy cream
2 quarts (½ gallon) whole milk
2 cups sugar (14 ounces)
3 vanilla beans, split and scraped
½ cup mint paste
½ cup Pistachio Paste (recipe below) or butter

MAKE GELATO

Heat cream, milk and scrapings from vanilla beans together in a heavy bottomed stockpot over medium heat, stirring occasionally, until just before boiling, about 195°F. Remove from heat.

In a large mixing bowl combine yolks with sugar, whisking together until thick and creamy.

Add the milk and cream mixture to the yolk mixture one ladle at a time, beating it in vigorously with the whisk. Repeat this several times until the yolk mixture feels warm. Pour the warmed-up yolk mixture slowly into the pot of milk and cream, beating with whisk. Add pistachio paste to milk and yolk mixture. Mix well. Pour contents of the pot into a bowl and refrigerate. Then put through a gelato machine following the machine instructions.

PISTACHIO PASTE

1 pound untoasted, unsalted pistachios
1 cup granulated sugar
½ cup water
1-2 tablespoons peanut or sunflower oil

Place the pistachios on a paper-lined pan, toast them for 15 minutes at 300°F degrees then let them cool down. Leave the sugar and the water in a saucepan on medium heat. When the sugar syrup reaches 250°F, add in the pistachios and stir for a few seconds. The pistachios will crystallize. When they are covered in sugar and almost no syrup is left in the saucepan, remove them and scatter them on parchment paper to cool down slightly. Place the pistachios in a food processor. Mix for about 2 minutes until you obtain a coarse mixture. Add 1-2 tablespoons peanut or sunflower oil. Keep mixing for about 10 minutes or until the mixture becomes a thick paste.

RABBIT GLACÉ

Makes 1 pint

10 pounds rabbit bones, cut into 2-inch pieces
¼ cup grapeseed oil
2 cups sliced onions
1 cup diced carrots
1 cup diced celery
1 cup sliced leeks
2 tablespoons tomato paste
2 cups white wine
2 sprigs thyme
1 tablespoon white peppercorns
2 bay leaves
2 tablespoons juniper berries
2 sprigs rosemary

Preheat oven to 375°F. Spread the rabbit bones in a single layer on 2 large cookie sheets and roast until golden brown, 30 to 45 minutes.

Meanwhile, place oil in a 10-quart stockpot over high heat. Add onions, carrots, celery and leeks and sauté until caramelized, 10 to 15 minutes. Add tomato paste and sauté until caramelized, 5 to 7 minutes. Add wine and reduce to the consistency of syrup.

Add roasted bones and the remaining ingredients and cover the bones with water.

Bring to a simmer over medium heat and skim the stock of all impurities and fats that rise to the top. Reduce heat to low and simmer, uncovered, for 5 hours, skimming every 30 minutes. Strain through a chinois, then return to heat and reduce to 1 pint. Strain again and chill.

ROASTED PEARS

Makes 6 half pears

3 Bartlett or Anjou pears
2 cups water
¼ cup sugar
2 tablespoons red wine
2 tablespoons honey
2 tablespoons grenadine
1 small whole red beet, peeled
1 bay leaf
1 cinnamon stick

Preheat oven to 375°F. Peel pears and cut in half. Scoop out seeds with a spoon. Roast for 25 to 28 minutes, until soft. In a saucepan large enough to accommodate pear halves in one layer, place remaining ingredients and stir. Add roasted pear halves to the liquid and bring to a gentle boil. Cook for 5 to 6 minutes, until liquid reaches the consistency of a light syrup, turning pears halfway through the cooking process. Remove from heat and allow to cool in refrigerator. Refrigerate pears in their liquid for up to 1 week.

**Note: We use this ingredient in several recipes, so you may want to consider doubling the batch for near-future use.*

FIRE-ROASTED RED BELL PEPPERS

As many red bell peppers as desired

Preheat grill to high and rinse peppers. Set peppers on hottest part of grill and cover grill. Turn peppers every 2 minutes or so as skin chars. When completely charred, after about 10 minutes, remove peppers from heat and transfer to a bowl. Cover with plastic wrap tightly to allow skins to loosen. Once cooled, peel off charred skin. Cut peppers in half and remove seeds. If desired, rinse and reserve for later use. Can be refrigerated for 4 to 5 days.

TOMATO–RED ONION MARMALADE

Makes 2 cups

1 large tomato
2 teaspoons grapeseed or canola oil
1 cup finely chopped red onion
¼ cup brown sugar
1 teaspoon white balsamic vinegar
½ cup tomato juice
4 cups water
1 teaspoon tomato paste
2 teaspoons liquid pectin
Salt, to taste
1 teaspoon black peppercorns
1 bay leaf
Zest of 1 orange
Zest of 1 lemon

Blanch tomato in boiling water for 10 seconds to easily remove peel. Chop to medium fineness to make about 1 cup. Place in a saucepan with oil, onion and sugar. Cook, stirring, over medium heat until sugar has dissolved, about 2 minutes. Add vinegar, tomato juice, water, tomato paste, pectin and salt. Use a 4-inch square of cheesecloth to create an herb sachet of peppercorns, bay leaf and zest. Secure with butcher's twine at top and add to pot. Simmer marmalade, stirring occasionally, for 2 to 2½ hours, until the consistency of jam. Let cool, then refrigerate. It improves after a couple of days, and can be stored in refrigerator for up to a month.

TOMATO SAUCE

Makes 1¾ quarts

2 large (28-ounce) cans San Marzano tomatoes
2–3 cloves garlic, shaved thin using a mandolin or knife
2 tablespoons julienned sweet basil
¼ cup extra-virgin olive oil
1 tablespoon sea salt
½ teaspoon freshly ground black pepper

Using a fine-mesh sieve, drain thin liquid from tomatoes, reserving sauce-like juices. Crush tomatoes by hand into small pieces less than ½ inch long. Place in a mixing bowl. Add remaining sauce from cans. Add garlic, basil, oil, salt and pepper and combine. Store in refrigerator for 5 to 7 days. When you need it, put in a sauté pan on medium heat and cook for 3-4 minutes.

TOMATO WATER

Makes 2 cups

1½ pounds tomatoes
1 cup fresh basil leaves
¼ cup fresh flat-leaf parsley leaves
2 medium shallots, chopped
2 cloves garlic, sliced
3 tablespoons white wine vinegar
1 tablespoon salt

Line a fine-mesh sieve with cheesecloth and set over a large bowl. Pulse tomatoes, shallots, garlic, basil, parsley, vinegar and salt in a food processor until coarsely chopped. Transfer mixture to the prepared sieve. Cover with plastic wrap and chill at least 12 hours. Do not stir or press on solids, or tomato water will be cloudy. Discard solids. Cover tomato water and chill.

Tomato water can be made up to 3 days in advance. Keep chilled.

VEAL JUS

Makes 4 cups

20 pounds veal knuckle bones, cut into 2-inch pieces
5 pounds veal feet, cut into 2-inch pieces
¼ cup grapeseed oil
4 cups onions, sliced

2 cups carrots, diced
2 cups celery, diced
2 cups leeks, sliced
2 cups celery root, diced
2 cups white mushrooms, sliced
½ cup tomato paste
4 cups red wine
10 sprigs thyme
25 black peppercorns
2 bay leaves
30 pounds ice cubes

Pre-heat the oven to 375°F. Spread the veal bones and feet in a single layer on 2 large rimmed baking sheets and roast in the oven until golden brown, approximately 45 minutes to 1 hour, turning the bones and feet after 30 minutes. Meanwhile, heat the oil in a 20-quart stockpot over high heat. Sauté the onions, carrots, celery, leeks and celery root until they caramelize, approximately 10 to 15 minutes. Add the mushrooms and sauté until soft. Add the tomato paste and sauté until caramelized, 5 to 7 minutes. Add the red wine and reduce to a syrup consistency. Add the thyme, peppercorns, bay leaves, bones and feet to the stockpot and cover with the ice. Bring to a simmer over medium heat and skim the stock of all impurities and fats that rise to the top. Simmer over low heat, uncovered, for 5 hours, skimming every 30 minutes. Strain through a fine-mesh chinois and return to the stove on medium heat to reduce to 1 quart. Strain again and chill over the ice.

VEAL STOCK

Makes 1 gallon

5 pounds veal bones
2 pounds veal tongue, cut into 2-inch pieces
3 pounds veal feet, cut into 2-inch pieces
20 pounds ice cubes, plus more for chilling
1 cup sliced onion
½ cup diced carrots
½ cup diced celery
½ cup diced celery root
½ cup diced leeks, white parts only
½ cup sliced button mushrooms
2 cups white wine
10 white peppercorns
5 sprigs thyme
1 bay leaf

Rinse bones well under running water for 5 minutes. Place the bones, tongue and feet in a 20-quart stockpot. Cover with 20 pounds ice and bring to a simmer over medium heat. Skim impurities and fats off the top, then add remaining ingredients. Simmer, uncovered, for 4 hours, skimming every 30 minutes. Strain stock through cheesecloth and chill over remaining ice.

VEGETABLE STOCK

Makes about 1 gallon, depending on simmer time

5 tablespoons grapeseed oil
1 cup sliced button mushrooms
1 cup diced leeks, white parts only
1 cup chopped carrot
1 cup chopped celery
1 cup chopped celery root
1 cup sliced shallots
1 cup chopped fennel, bulb only
1 cup sliced white onion
Pinch of salt
1½ gallons cold water
5 white peppercorns
3 bay leaves
1 (6-inch) sprig thyme

Heat oil in a 20-quart stockpot over medium heat. Add all vegetables with a pinch of salt. Stir to sweat the vegetables, cooking for 10 minutes or until vegetables soften. Add remaining ingredients and simmer for 1¼ to 1½ hours. Strain through a chinois or fine-mesh sieve. Store in refrigerator for up to 1 week, or freeze by cupfuls in small bags or containers for future use.

VENISON GLACE

Makes 1½ to 2 cups

STOCK

10 pounds venison bones
¼ cup grapeseed oil
2 pounds carrots, coarsely chopped
2 pounds celery, coarsely chopped
2 pounds red onions, coarsely chopped
⅓ cup tomato paste
4 cups ice cubes
4 (5-inch) sprigs rosemary
4 (5-inch) sprigs thyme
¼ cup whole black peppercorns
¼ cup juniper berries, slightly crushed
3 bay leaves

WINE SYRUP

½ bottle red wine
¼ cup sugar
2 (5-inch) sprigs rosemary
6 cloves garlic, crushed

PREPARE STOCK

Preheat oven to 375°F. Rinse bones under water and lay on baking sheets. Roast bones until golden brown.

Meanwhile, in a large stockpot over medium heat, place oil, carrots, celery and onions. Cook until onions are translucent. Stir in tomato paste and cook for 1 minute. Add ice and roasted bones to stockpot, followed by remaining ingredients.

Add enough water to cover bones. Bring stock to a gentle boil, then lower heat to maintain a simmer. Cook for 5 to 6 hours, until liquid has reduced below level of bones. Strain the liquid into another pot, discarding bones and vegetables. Return stock to heat and reduce liquid to one-fifth.

PREPARE WINE SYRUP

In a saucepan, combine all ingredients. Bring to a simmer and reduce until the consistency of syrup. Stir syrup into stock, then pass through a fine-mesh sieve.

Store glace in refrigerator for up to 1 week.

MY TEAM
the Best

Clockwise, from top left: Executive Chef Jason Goddard, General Manager Tanya Buchanan, Wine Sommelier Liset Zelaya and Chief Operating Officer Lili Montes

I want to thank my management team: five special people who work hard and loyally to make our restaurants the successes they have become. Without them, I would not have made this cookbook for you. I would not be opening our doors every day. They make it possible for me to do my best as a chef and restaurant owner.

In the restaurant business, there is always a lot of staff turnover, so you need a strong management team you can count on to keep control of standards when there is a change in staffing. I always say, "My dishwasher and my general manager are equally important; they just have different responsibilities." Everybody must work together for the complicated machinery of a restaurant to run smoothly.

I am so grateful to them, starting with my beautiful wife, Ingrid, who makes our guests feel so warmly welcomed and runs interference for our managers. She really makes everybody look good.

My executive chef, Jason Goddard, has been running the Sea Salt kitchen calmly and capably for five years. He has many great talents, and prime among them is understanding me. Raised on a sustainable farm in Iowa and trained in culinary skills at an early age, he has my instinct for the finest quality in food.

At the front of the house, Tanya Buchanan has been general manager for two years. She came to us from a Michelin-rated Las Vegas restaurant group, and understands the operation of a fine restaurant. She was particularly helpful in getting me organized to complete this cookbook, so a big thanks to her for that.

My wine sommelier, Liset Zelaya, has worked at Sea Salt for four years, and during that time has managed to make our wine cellar one of the best if not the best in the region. She loves wine as much as I do, which is saying a lot, and it really shows.

Behind the scenes, Lili Montes, our chief operating officer, makes it all happen by managing office matters. She has been with us for five years, making sure bills get paid, deposits get made and books are in balance. So she saves me from a lot of the minutia of running a business.

I cannot emphasize enough how important my wonderful management team is to me and my restaurants. I know I don't thank them enough, so I dedicate this to them with gratitude for their work ethics and loyalty.

Acknowledgments

We have unlimited gratitude for the many good people who have helped us along the way and not nearly enough space to list them all. A short list:

Bruce Gilbert, president of D. Garrett Construction, who made the impossible possible—from building permit to certificate of occupancy in 87 days. A record-breaker for construction in Naples ... or anywhere for that matter. Thanks, too, for answering our call when we decided to build additional restaurants.

Kathleen Passidomo, attorney and member of the Florida House of Representatives. Thanks for being our "consigliere" and dear friend. Your advice has been invaluable.

Barbara Walker and David Vaughn: Thank your for your support and friendship from Washington, D.C., to Naples. Your invitation to visit you in Naples ignited our attraction to this lovely city and led to our prime location for Sea Salt on Third Street South.

Colman Andrews, gourmand and writer extraordinaire. Thanks for sharing your passion for food and for writing the foreword for this book.

John Mariani: Thanks for your many years of support, starting with our first restaurant, Goldoni, in Washington, D.C. Your naming Sea Salt one of *Esquire's* "Best New Restaurants of 2009" helped to put Sea Salt and Naples on the culinary map.

Dean Corsones and Paula Polito: No words can even begin to express our gratitude for your friendship, support and mentorship.

Bob Morris, our publisher, his lovely wife, Debbie, and the whole Story Farm team: Thank you for your devotion and vision, which helped put this book together.

INDEX

Numbers in **bold** indicate pages with photos

A

Aielli, Fabrizio
  cooking at Sea Salt by, 1
  cooking career of, 1, 4–6
  cooking style of, 4–5, 6
  day in the life of, 6
  early life of, 4, 117, 145
  marriage of, 4
  move to America by, 1, 4
  move to Naples, 1
  passion for food of, 2, 5–6
  pride and happiness of, 6
Aielli, Ingrid
  cooking of, 154
  marriage of, 4
  move to America by, 1, 4
  move to Naples, 1
Akaushi beef, 145
  Akaushi Beef Tenderloin with Asparagus, Morel and Red Pepper-Date Sauce, **146,** 147
Alaea red clay salt, 13
Anchovies
  Evolution of Caesar Salad, 58, **59**
Appetizers and first impressions, 17
  Beef Carpaccio and Ubriaco Cheese, with Tropical Truffle and Tequila-Jalapeño Sauce, **28,** 29
  Calamari with Portobello Cappuccino and Quail Egg, **18,** 19
  Cuttlefish with Black-Burn Onion Sauce, Pickled Celery and Radish, 32, **33**
  Foie Gras Peanut Butter Terrine with Balsamic Must and Raspberry Jelly, 30, **31**
  Kumamoto Oysters on a Foggy Day in Venice, 22, **23**
  Mazara del Vallo Prawns in Orange Sauce with Salmon Roe and French Beans, **36,** 37
  Octopus in Crustacean Sauce with Raisin Tomatoes, Smoked Potatoes and Summer Truffle Jam, **34,** 35
  Prosciutto, Figs and Arugula with Tomato Marmalade and Parmesan Crisps, **20,** 21
  Sea Urchin, Lobster and Scallops with Braised Potato and Lardo, 26, **27**
Apples
  Green Apple Soufflé, 184, **185**
Apricots
  Guinea Hen with Black Garlic, Egg Yolk Truffle and Apricot Sauce, 158, **159**
Arugula, 41
  Bread Leaves with Prosciutto, Pecorino and Arugula, 168, **169**
  Prosciutto, Figs and Arugula with Tomato Marmalade and Parmesan Crisps, **20,** 21
  Watermelon Gazpacho with Guanciale, Feta and Arugula Sorbet, **68,** 69
Asparagus
  Akaushi Beef Tenderloin with Asparagus, Morel and Red Pepper-Date Sauce, **146,** 147
  Guinea Hen with Black Garlic, Egg Yolk Truffle and Apricot Sauce, 158, **159**
  Kale, Persimmon and Pomegranate with Olive Oil Emulsion and Champagne Vinegar Gelée, 60, **61**
  Monkfish and Corn Pudding with Eggplant, Asparagus and Morels, 138, **139**

B

Bacon, pancetta, lardo, and guanciale
  Bigoli and Octopus with Amatriciana Sauce, **104,** 105
  Saffron Taglierini Carbonara with Sea Urchin and Guanciale, 2, **110,** 111
  Salt Cave–Aged Rib-Eye Steak with Cocoa Nibs and Bacon–Celery Root Brûlée, **160,** 161
  Sea Urchin, Lobster and Scallops with Braised Potato and Lardo, 26, **27**
  Watermelon Gazpacho with Guanciale, Feta and Arugula Sorbet, **68,** 69
Barbatella
  changes at, 5–6
  desserts at, 183
  menu at, 1, 5
  opening of, 1, 5
  wine at, 207
Bar noshes, 167. See also Sandwiches
Beef, 145
  Akaushi Beef Tenderloin with Asparagus, Morel and Red Pepper-Date Sauce, **146,** 147
  Beef Carpaccio and Ubriaco Cheese, with Tropical Truffle and Tequila-Jalapeño Sauce, **28,** 29
  Beef Jus, 208
  Beef Stock, 208
  Kobe Burgers with King Crab Tempura, 176, **177**
  Salt Cave–Aged Rib-Eye Steak with Cocoa Nibs and Bacon–Celery Root Brûlée, **160,** 161
Beets
  Duck Breast with Sevruga Caviar, Kumamoto Oysters, Chive-Honey Sour Cream and Roots, **150,** 151
  Honeyed Beet and Peach Salad with Whipped Goat Cheese, Sunflower Seed Praline and Raspberry Vinaigrette, **44,** 45
  Red Beet Gnocchi with Hazelnut, Speck and Ricotta Salata, **84,** 85
  Turbot with Lobster Milk Shake, Gold Beets and Warm Green Pea Mayonnaise, **124,** 125
  Venison Tenderloin with Chestnut Grappa Sauce and Braised Root Vegetables, 152, **153**
  Watermelon Gazpacho with Guanciale, Feta and Arugula Sorbet, 68, 69
Blueberries
  Blueberry Bulleit, 205, **205**

Lemony Polenta-Stuffed Cappellacci with Rabbit and Blueberry Sauces, **88,** 89
Brining, 145
Brined Kurobuta Pork Chops with Black Cherry Sauce and Summer Vegetables, 148, **149**
Meat & Poultry Brine, 208
Venison Tenderloin with Chestnut Grappa Sauce and Braised Root Vegetables, 152, **153**
Brussels sprouts
Mussels and Brussels with Duck Wing Broth, 70, **71**
Rack of Lamb with Peppermint Emulsion, Rosemary Juice, Purple Potato and Brussels Leaves, 162, **163**
Buchanan, Tanya, 216, **216**
Bulifant, Susan, 141

C

Cabbage
Crunchy Chicken with Jalapeño Cabbage Slaw, Saffron Aïoli and Sriracha Mayo, 167, **174,** 175
Calamari with Portobello Cappuccino and Quail Egg, **18,** 19
California cuisine, 4–5
Cardoons
Chicken Velouté with Rosemary Brioche and Cardoon Spread, 74, **75**
Carrots
Brined Kurobuta Pork Chops with Black Cherry Sauce and Summer Vegetables, 148, **149**
Chocolate Ravioli Stuffed with Roasted Carrot and Amaretti on Quail Ragu, **94,** 95
Duck Breast with Sevruga Caviar, Kumamoto Oysters, Chive-Honey Sour Cream and Roots, **150,** 151
Venison Tenderloin with Chestnut Grappa Sauce and Braised Root Vegetables, 152, **153**
Caviar
Duck Breast with Sevruga Caviar, Kumamoto Oysters, Chive-Honey Sour Cream and Roots, **150,** 151
Potato and Leek Soup with Crème Fraîche, Caviar and Quail Egg, 76, **77**
Celery
Cuttlefish with Black-Burn Onion Sauce, Pickled Celery and Radish, 32, **33**
Fried Grouper with Tomato–Red Onion Marmalade and Pickled Celery, **170,** 171
Pickled Celery, 211
Celery root
Salt Cave–Aged Rib-Eye Steak with Cocoa Nibs and Bacon–Celery Root Brûlée, **160,** 161
Venison Tenderloin with Chestnut Grappa Sauce and Braised Root Vegetables, 152, **153**
Cheese
Beef Carpaccio and Ubriaco Cheese, with Tropical Truffle and Tequila-Jalapeño Sauce, **28,** 29
Endive and Frisée Popcorn Salad with Roasted Pear, Piave Cheese and Black Truffle, 42, **43**
Honeyed Beet and Peach Salad with Whipped Goat Cheese, Sunflower Seed Praline and Raspberry Vinaigrette, **44,** 45
Lobster Reuben, 167, **178,** 179
Mezzelune and Stracchino with Venus Clams, Soppressata and Fava Beans, 106, **107**
Radicchio and Strawberry Salad with Gorgonzola-Pistachio Truffles and Treviso, **46,** 47
Watermelon Gazpacho with Guanciale, Feta and Arugula Sorbet, **68,** 69
See also Mozzarella and burrata; Parmesan cheese; Ricotta cheese; Ricotta salata
Cherries
Brined Kurobuta Pork Chops with Black Cherry Sauce and Summer Vegetables, 148, **149**
Lola Cherry Cola, 205, **205**
Smoked Cherry Soup with Farro and Wild Boar Sausage, **72,** 73
Chestnuts
Venison Tenderloin with Chestnut Grappa Sauce and Braised Root Vegetables, 152, **153**
Chicken, 145
Best Chicken Ever 'Nilde," 154, **154–55**
Chicken Stock, 209
Chicken Velouté with Rosemary Brioche and Cardoon Spread, 74, 75
Crunchy Chicken with Jalapeño Cabbage Slaw, Saffron Aïoli and Sriracha Mayo, 167, **174,** 175
Chocolate
Chocolate Ravioli Stuffed with Roasted Carrot and Amaretti on Quail Ragu, **94,** 95
Hot Chocolate, Murray River Salt, Caramel, **186,** 187
Menta Gelato with Three-Chocolate Brittle, **194,** 195
Clams
Mezzelune and Stracchino with Venus Clams, Soppressata and Fava Beans, 106, **107**
Cocktails, 203
Blueberry Bulleit, 205, **205**
Italian Summer, 205, **205**
Lola Cherry Cola, 205, **205**
Mandarine Mojito, 205, **205**
Naples Negroni, 205, **205**
Peach Kiss, 206, **206**
Sea Salt Bloody Mary, 13, 203, 204–5, **204**
Sea Salt Margarita, 206, **206**
Sea Salt Sidecar, 206, **206**
Seaside Lemonade, 206, **206**
Cocoa nibs
Salt Cave–Aged Rib-Eye Steak with Cocoa Nibs and Bacon–Celery Root Brûlée, **160,** 161
Cooking
common sense and, 67

creative process of, 2, 10
deciding what to cook, 4
enjoyment of, 10
flash-cooking, 10
freedom of travel and, 4–5, 6
with a glass of wine and smile on your face, 4
at-home techniques, 6, 10
simplicity of cooking from the heart, 2
stressing about, 2, 4
Corn
Brined Kurobuta Pork Chops with Black Cherry Sauce and Summer Vegetables, 148, **149**
Monkfish and Corn Pudding with Eggplant, Asparagus and Morels, 138, **139**
Crab legs
Kobe Burgers with King Crab Tempura, 176, **177**
Crème fraîche, 209
Potato and Leek Soup with Crème Fraîche, Caviar and Quail Egg, 76, **77**
Cucumbers
Watermelon Gazpacho with Guanciale, Feta and Arugula Sorbet, **68,** 69
Cuttlefish
Black Ink Cuttlefish Risotto with Baked Sheep Ricotta and Fava Beans, 108, **109**
Cuttlefish with Black-Burn Onion Sauce, Pickled Celery and Radish, 32, 33

D

Dates
Akaushi Beef Tenderloin with Asparagus, Morel and Red Pepper-Date Sauce, **146,** 147
Date Crème Brûlée with Kahlúa, 196, **197**
Desserts and sweet endings, 183
Date Crème Brûlée with Kahlúa, 196, **197**
Green Apple Soufflé, 184, **185**
Hot Chocolate, Murray River Salt, Caramel, **186,** 187
Lemon Sorbet with Mango-Fennel Salsa, 190, **190–91**
Menta Gelato with Three-Chocolate Brittle, **194,** 195
Roasted Pear Soup with Chianti–Black Pepper Sorbet, 192, **193**
Strawberry and Balsamic Mascarpone Gelato with Pink Peppercorns and Mint, **188,** 189
Watermelon, Berry, Pistachio Halva Salad, **198,** 199
Duck
Duck Breast with Sevruga Caviar, Kumamoto Oysters, Chive-Honey Sour Cream and Roots, **150,** 151
Duck Wing Stock, 209
Mussels and Brussels with Duck Wing Broth, 70, **71**

E

Eggplants
Monkfish and Corn Pudding with Eggplant, Asparagus and Morels, 138, **139**
Eggs
Calamari with Portobello Cappuccino and Quail Egg, **18,** 19
Guinea Hen with Black Garlic, Egg Yolk Truffle and Apricot Sauce, 158, **159**
Potato and Leek Soup with Crème Fraîche, Caviar and Quail Egg, 76, **77**
Endive, 41
Endive and Frisée Popcorn Salad with Roasted Pear, Piave Cheese and Black Truffle, 42, **43**
Espresso brava salt, 13

F

Farro
Smoked Cherry Soup with Farro and Wild Boar Sausage, **72,** 73
Fava beans
Black Ink Cuttlefish Risotto with Baked Sheep Ricotta and Fava Beans, 108, **109**
John Dory with Garden Peas and Prosecco Nage, **130,** 131
Mezzelune and Stracchino with Venus Clams, Soppressata and Fava Beans, 106, **107**
Pan-Seared Black Grouper with Black Truffle Butter, Fava Beans and Smoked-Salt Fingerling Potatoes, 132, **133**
Fennel bulb
Fennel and Orange with Pickled Red Onions and Black Sambuca Dressing, **52,** 53
Lemon Sorbet with Mango-Fennel Salsa, 190, **190–91**
Figs
Black Cod Fillet with Black Truffle, Serrano Ham, Figs and Amarone Zabaglione, 134, **135**
Prosciutto, Figs and Arugula with Tomato Marmalade and Parmesan Crisps, **20,** 21
Fish, 117
Black Cod Fillet with Black Truffle, Serrano Ham, Figs and Amarone Zabaglione, 134, **135**
Duck Fat–Poached Ahi Tuna with Orange Moscato Nectar, Foie Gras Stracciatella, Salsify Puree, **136,** 137
Fish Fumet, 209
Fried Grouper with Tomato–Red Onion Marmalade and Pickled Celery, **170,** 171
Halibut with Rhubarb-Strawberry Sauce, 118, **119**
John Dory with Garden Peas and Prosecco Nage, **130,** 131
Monkfish and Corn Pudding with Eggplant, Asparagus and Morels, 138, **139**
Ôra King Salmon with Beluga Lentils, Baby Turnips and Mustard Sauce, **120,** 121
Pan-Seared Black Grouper with Black Truffle Butter, Fava Beans and Smoked-Salt Fingerling Potatoes, 132, **133**
Turbot with Lobster Milk Shake, Gold Beets and Warm Green Pea Mayonnaise, **124,** 125
Vanilla Salt-Crusted Branzino with Blood Orange Sauce and Campari Cipollini, 126, **127**
wine to drink with, 117
Fish Lady, 141

Flor blanca, 13
Foie gras
Duck Fat–Poached Ahi Tuna with Orange Moscato Nectar, Foie Gras Stracciatella, Salsify Puree, **136,** 137
Foie Gras Peanut Butter Terrine with Balsamic Must and Raspberry Jelly, 30, **31**

G

Garlic
Guinea Hen with Black Garlic, Egg Yolk Truffle and Apricot Sauce, 158, **159**
Garnishes, 10
Gelato and sorbet, 41, 183
Lemon Sorbet with Mango-Fennel Salsa, 190, **190–91**
Menta Gelato with Three-Chocolate Brittle, **194,** 195
Strawberry and Balsamic Mascarpone Gelato with Pink Peppercorns and Mint, **188,** 189
Ghost pepper salt, 13
Ginger salt, Thai, 13
Global cuisine, 4–5
Goddard, Jason, 6, 141, 216, **216**
Goldoni, 1, 5
Goldoni, Carlo, 1, 5
Grappa
Chamomile-Langoustine Risotto with Grappa and Lemon, 86, **87**
Venison Tenderloin with Chestnut Grappa Sauce and Braised Root Vegetables, 152, **153**
Grass-fed beef, 145
Green beans
John Dory with Garden Peas and Prosecco Nage, **130,** 131
Mazara del Vallo Prawns in Orange Sauce with Salmon Roe and French Beans, **36,** 37
Green tea (matcha) salt, 13
Guanciale
Saffron Taglierini Carbonara with Sea Urchin and Guanciale, 2, **110,** 111
Watermelon Gazpacho with Guanciale, Feta and Arugula Sorbet, **68,** 69
Guinea Hen with Black Garlic, Egg Yolk Truffle and Apricot Sauce, 158, **159**

H

Ham
Black Cod Fillet with Black Truffle, Serrano Ham, Figs and Amarone Zabaglione, 134, **135**
Hazelnuts
Red Beet Gnocchi with Hazelnut, Speck and Ricotta Salata, **84,** 85
Hearts of palm
Beef Carpaccio and Ubriaco Cheese, with Tropical Truffle and Tequila-Jalapeño Sauce, **28,** 29
Herban Gardens, 62
Herbs, garnishing with, 10
Himalayan pink salt, 13, 145

I

Ingredients
buying ready-made items, 10
fresh ingredients and California cuisine, 4–5
produce and microgreens, 62
quality of, 10, 113, 203
substitutions, 2, 10
weighing and measuring, 10

J

Jalapeños
Beef Carpaccio and Ubriaco Cheese, with Tropical Truffle and Tequila-Jalapeño Sauce, **28,** 29
Crunchy Chicken with Jalapeño Cabbage Slaw, Saffron Aïoli and Sriracha Mayo, 167, **174,** 175
Watermelon Gazpacho with Guanciale, Feta and Arugula Sorbet, **68,** 69
Jams and jellies
Balsamic Jelly, 48, **49**
Champagne Vinegar Gelée, 60, **61**
Raspberry Jelly, 30, **31**
Summer Truffle Jam, **34,** 35
Tomato–Red Onion Marmalade, **170,** 171, 214–15

K

Kala namak, 13
Kale, 41
Kale, Persimmon and Pomegranate with Olive Oil Emulsion and Champagne Vinegar Gelée, 60, **61**
Kennedy, John F., 13

Lamb
Rack of Lamb with Peppermint Emulsion, Rosemary Juice, Purple Potato and Brussels Leaves, 162, **163**

L

Langoustines
Chamomile-Langoustine Risotto with Grappa and Lemon, 86, **87**
Lardo
Sea Urchin, Lobster and Scallops with Braised Potato and Lardo, 26, **27**
Leeks
Potato and Leek Soup with Crème Fraîche, Caviar and Quail Egg, 76, **77**
Lemons and lemon juice
Lemon Sorbet with Mango-Fennel Salsa, 190, **190–91**
Lemony Polenta-Stuffed Cappellacci with Rabbit and Blueberry Sauces, **88,** 89
Seaside Lemonade, 206, **206**
Lentils
Ôra King Salmon with Beluga Lentils, Baby Turnips and Mustard Sauce, **120,** 121
Lime fresco salt, 13
Limes and lime juice
Mandarine Mojito, 205, **205**

Sea Salt Margarita, 206, **206**
Lobster
Lobster Reuben, 167, **178,** 179
Lobster Risotto with Roasted Tomato and White Truffle Perfume, **98,** 99
Lobster Stock, 210
Octopus in Crustacean Sauce with Raisin Tomatoes, Smoked Potatoes and Summer Truffle Jam, **34,** 35
Pappardelle and Lobster with Hen of the Woods and Egg Yolk, **92,** 93
Sea Urchin, Lobster and Scallops with Braised Potato and Lardo, 26, **27**
Turbot with Lobster Milk Shake, Gold Beets and Warm Green Pea Mayonnaise, **124,** 125
Love, Norman, 183

M

Mangos
Lemon Sorbet with Mango-Fennel Salsa, 190, **190–91**
Sea Salt Sidecar, 206, **206**
Maple sea salt, Vermont, 13
Matcha (green tea) salt, 13
Mayan sun salt, 13
Mayonnaise, 210
Crunchy Chicken with Jalapeño Cabbage Slaw, Saffron Aïoli and Sriracha Mayo, **174,** 175
Turbot with Lobster Milk Shake, Gold Beets and Warm Green Pea Mayonnaise, **124,** 125
Microgreens, 62
Montes, Lili, 216, **216**
Mozzarella and burrata
Crazy Bubbling Tomato with Burratina and Green Pea Shoots, **50,** 51
Deconstructed Tomatoes with Balsamic Jelly and Liquid Buffalo Mozzarella, 48, **49**
Inside-Out Tortelli, Burrata, Honey, Mint, Shrimp, 100, **101**
Murray River pink salt flakes, 13, 183
Hot Chocolate, Murray River Salt, Caramel, **186,** 187
Mushrooms
Akaushi Beef Tenderloin with Asparagus, Morel and Red Pepper-Date Sauce, **146,** 147
Calamari with Portobello Cappuccino and Quail Egg, **18,** 19
Monkfish and Corn Pudding with Eggplant, Asparagus and Morels, 138, **139**
Pappardelle and Lobster with Hen of the Woods and Egg Yolk, **92,** 93
Mussels and Brussels with Duck Wing Broth, 70, **71**

N

Naples, 1, 5
New American cuisine, 4–5

O

Ocean, salt in our blood and ties to the, 13
Octopus
Bigoli and Octopus with Amatriciana Sauce, **104,** 105
Octopus in Crustacean Sauce with Raisin Tomatoes, Smoked Potatoes and Summer Truffle Jam, **34,** 35
Olives
Best Chicken Ever 'Nilde," 154, **154–55**
Onions
Cuttlefish with Black-Burn Onion Sauce, Pickled Celery and Radish, 32, **33**
Fennel and Orange with Pickled Red Onions and Black Sambuca Dressing, **52,** 53
Fried Grouper with Tomato–Red Onion Marmalade and Pickled Celery, **170,** 171
John Dory with Garden Peas and Prosecco Nage, **130,** 131
Pickled Red Onions, 211
Tomato–Red Onion Marmalade, 212
Vanilla Salt-Crusted Branzino with Blood Orange Sauce and Campari Cipollini, 126, **127**
Oranges and orange juice
Duck Fat–Poached Ahi Tuna with Orange Moscato Nectar, Foie Gras Stracciatella, Salsify Puree, **136,** 137
Fennel and Orange with Pickled Red Onions and Black Sambuca Dressing, **52,** 53
Mazara del Vallo Prawns in Orange Sauce with Salmon Roe and French Beans, **36,** 37
Orange Nectar, 210
Vanilla Salt-Crusted Branzino with Blood Orange Sauce and Campari Cipollini, 126, **127**
Osteria Goldoni, 1, 5
Oysters
Duck Breast with Sevruga Caviar, Kumamoto Oysters, Chive-Honey Sour Cream and Roots, **150,** 151
Kumamoto Oysters on a Foggy Day in Venice, 22, **23**
preparation of at Sea Salt restaurants, 1, 5

P

Pancetta. See Bacon, pancetta, lardo, and guanciale
Parmesan cheese
Evolution of Caesar Salad, 58, **59**
Prosciutto, Figs and Arugula with Tomato Marmalade and Parmesan Crisps, **20,** 21
Pasta, 83
Bigoli and Octopus with Amatriciana Sauce, **104,** 105
Chocolate Ravioli Stuffed with Roasted Carrot and Amaretti on Quail Ragu, **94,** 95
Lemony Polenta-Stuffed Cappellacci with Rabbit and Blueberry Sauces, **88,** 89
Mezzelune and Stracchino with Venus Clams, Soppressata and Fava Beans, 106, **107**
Pappardelle and Lobster with Hen of the Woods and Egg Yolk, **92,** 93
Pasta Dough, 210
Red Beet Gnocchi with Hazelnut, Speck and Ricotta Salata, **84,** 85
Saffron Taglierini Carbonara with Sea Urchin and Guanciale, 2, **110,** 111
Inside-Out Tortelli, Burrata, Honey, Mint, Shrimp, 100, **101**
Pasta machines, 10
Peaches
Honeyed Beet and Peach Salad with Whipped Goat Cheese,

Sunflower Seed Praline and Raspberry Vinaigrette, **44,** 45
Peach Kiss, 206, **206**
Peanut butter
Foie Gras Peanut Butter Terrine with Balsamic Must and Raspberry Jelly, 30, **31**
Pears
Endive and Frisée Popcorn Salad with Roasted Pear, Piave Cheese and Black Truffle, 42, **43**
Roasted Pears, 212
Roasted Pear Soup with Chianti–Black Pepper Sorbet, 192, **193**
Peas and pea pods, 67
Brined Kurobuta Pork Chops with Black Cherry Sauce and Summer Vegetables, 148, **149**
John Dory with Garden Peas and Prosecco Nage, **130,** 131
Pea Puree, 211
Sweet Pea Soup with Roasted Ricotta, Speck and Honeysuckle, **78,** 79
Turbot with Lobster Milk Shake, Gold Beets and Warm Green Pea Mayonnaise, **124,** 125
Pea shoots
Crazy Bubbling Tomato with Burratina and Green Pea Shoots, **50,** 51
Peppers
Akaushi Beef Tenderloin with Asparagus, Morel and Red Pepper-Date Sauce, **146,** 147
Best Chicken Ever 'Nilde,' 154, **154–55**
Fire-Roasted Red Bell Peppers, 214
Persimmons
Kale, Persimmon and Pomegranate with Olive Oil Emulsion and Champagne Vinegar Gelée, 60, **61**
Kumamoto Oysters on a Foggy Day in Venice, 22, **23**
Pheasant, 145
Pink salt, 13, 145
Pistachios
Radicchio and Strawberry Salad with Gorgonzola-Pistachio Truffles and Treviso, **46,** 47
Watermelon, Berry, Pistachio Halva Salad, **198,** 199
Polenta
Lemony Polenta-Stuffed Cappellacci with Rabbit and Blueberry Sauces, **88,** 89
Pomegranate juice and seeds
Kale, Persimmon and Pomegranate with Olive Oil Emulsion and Champagne Vinegar Gelée, 60, **61**
Kumamoto Oysters on a Foggy Day in Venice, 22, **23**
Popcorn
Endive and Frisée Popcorn Salad with Roasted Pear, Piave Cheese and Black Truffle, 42, **43**
Pork, 145
Brined Kurobuta Pork Chops with Black Cherry Sauce and Summer Vegetables, 148, **149**
Potatoes
Octopus in Crustacean Sauce with Raisin Tomatoes, Smoked Potatoes and Summer Truffle Jam, **34,** 35
Pan-Seared Black Grouper with Black Truffle Butter, Fava Beans and Smoked-Salt Fingerling Potatoes, 132, **133**
Potato and Leek Soup with Crème Fraîche, Caviar and Quail Egg, 76, **77**
Rack of Lamb with Peppermint Emulsion, Rosemary Juice, Purple Potato and Brussels Leaves, 162, **163**
Sea Urchin, Lobster and Scallops with Braised Potato and Lardo, 26, 27
Prawns. See Shrimp and prawns
Prosciutto
Bread Leaves with Prosciutto, Pecorino and Arugula, 168, **169**
Prosciutto, Figs and Arugula with Tomato Marmalade and Parmesan Crisps, **20,** 21
Pyramid salt, 13

Q

Quail
Chocolate Ravioli Stuffed with Roasted Carrot and Amaretti on Quail Ragu, **94,** 95

R

Rabbit, 145
Lemony Polenta-Stuffed Cappellacci with Rabbit and Blueberry Sauces, **88,** 89
Rabbit Glace, 211-12
Radicchio, 41
Radicchio and Strawberry Salad with Gorgonzola-Pistachio Truffles and Treviso, **46,** 47
Radishes
Cuttlefish with Black-Burn Onion Sauce, Pickled Celery and Radish, 32, **33**
Raspberries and raspberry juice
Berry Juice, 208
Foie Gras Peanut Butter Terrine with Balsamic Must and Raspberry Jelly, 30, **31**
Honeyed Beet and Peach Salad with Whipped Goat Cheese, Sunflower Seed Praline and Raspberry Vinaigrette, **44,** 45
Seaside Lemonade, 206, **206**
Watermelon, Berry, Pistachio Halva Salad, **198,** 199
Recipes
changes to, 2, 4, 6, 10
inspirations for and creation of, 2, 4, 5
not using, 6, 9, 10
stories and memories connected to, 2
writing down and following, 2
Rhubarb
Halibut with Rhubarb-Strawberry Sauce, 118, **119**
Rice
Black Ink Cuttlefish Risotto with Baked Sheep Ricotta and Fava Beans, 108, **109**
Chamomile-Langoustine Risotto with Grappa and Lemon, 86, **87**
Lobster Risotto with Roasted Tomato and White Truffle Perfume, **98,** 99
Ricotta cheese
Black Ink Cuttlefish Risotto with Baked Sheep Ricotta and Fava Beans, 108, **109**
Red Beet Gnocchi with Hazelnut, Speck and Ricotta Salata, **84,** 85
Ricotta salata
Red Beet Gnocchi with Hazelnut, Speck and Ricotta Salata, **84,** 85

Sweet Pea Soup with Roasted Ricotta, Speck and Honeysuckle, **78,** 79
Romaine lettuce, 41
Evolution of Caesar Salad, 58, **59**
Rose salt, 13
Ryan, Ken, 62

S

Salads, 41
Crazy Bubbling Tomato with Burratina and Green Pea Shoots, **50,** 51
Deconstructed Tomatoes with Balsamic Jelly and Liquid Buffalo Mozzarella, 48, **49**
Endive and Frisée Popcorn Salad with Roasted Pear, Piave Cheese and Black Truffle, 42, **43**
Evolution of Caesar Salad, 58, **59**
Fennel and Orange with Pickled Red Onions and Black Sambuca Dressing, **52,** 53
Honeyed Beet and Peach Salad with Whipped Goat Cheese, Sunflower Seed Praline and Raspberry Vinaigrette, **44,** 45
Kale, Persimmon and Pomegranate with Olive Oil Emulsion and Champagne Vinegar Gelée, 60, **61**
Radicchio and Strawberry Salad with Gorgonzola-Pistachio Truffles and Treviso, **46,** 47
Salmon roe
Mazara del Vallo Prawns in Orange Sauce with Salmon Roe and French Beans, **36,** 37
Salsify
Duck Fat–Poached Ahi Tuna with Orange Moscato Nectar, Foie Gras Stracciatella, Salsify Puree, **136,** 137
Salt in our blood and ties to the ocean, 13
Salts
amount used in the kitchen and retail shop, 13
artisanal salts, 13
healthful, healing properties of, 13, 145
infused salts, 13
land foundation salts, 13
number of varieties used by Fabrizio, 1, 13
sea salts, 1, 13
use of in cooking, 13
Sambuca
Fennel and Orange with Pickled Red Onions and Black Sambuca Dressing, 52, 53
Lemon Sorbet with Mango-Fennel Salsa, 190, **190–91**
Sandwiches, 167
Bread Leaves with Prosciutto, Pecorino and Arugula, 168, **169**
Crunchy Chicken with Jalapeño Cabbage Slaw, Saffron Aïoli and Sriracha Mayo, 167, **174,** 175
Fried Grouper with Tomato–Red Onion Marmalade and Pickled Celery, 170, 171
Kobe Burgers with King Crab Tempura, 176, 177
Lobster Reuben, 167, **178,** 179
Sauerkraut
Lobster Reuben, 167, **178,** 179
Sausage
Mezzelune and Stracchino with Venus Clams, Soppressata and Fava Beans, 106, **107**
Smoked Cherry Soup with Farro and Wild Boar Sausage, **72,** 73
Scallops
Sea Urchin, Lobster and Scallops with Braised Potato and Lardo, 26, **27**
Sea Salt, Naples
changes at, 5–6
cooking by Fabrizio at, 1, 6
day in the life of a chef, 6
desserts at, 183
inspiration for, 13
menu at, 1, 5, 6
opening of, 1, 5
popularity of, 1
talking to guests at, 6
wine at, 207
Sea Salt, St. Petersburg, 5
Sea urchins
Saffron Taglierini Carbonara with Sea Urchin and Guanciale, 2, **110,** 111
Sea Urchin, Lobster and Scallops with Braised Potato and Lardo, 26, **27**
Sel de mer, 13
Sel gris, 13
Shrimp and prawns
Mazara del Vallo Prawns in Orange Sauce with Salmon Roe and French Beans, **36,** 37
Octopus in Crustacean Sauce with Raisin Tomatoes, Smoked Potatoes and Summer Truffle Jam, **34,** 35
Inside-Out Tortelli, Burrata, Honey, Mint, Shrimp, 100, **101**
wild shrimp, 141
Sorbet. See Gelato and sorbet
Soup, 67
Chicken Velouté with Rosemary Brioche and Cardoon Spread, 74, **75**
Mussels and Brussels with Duck Wing Broth, 70, **71**
Potato and Leek Soup with Crème Fraîche, Caviar and Quail Egg, 76, **77**
Smoked Cherry Soup with Farro and Wild Boar Sausage, **72,** 73
Sweet Pea Soup with Roasted Ricotta, Speck and Honeysuckle, **78,** 79
Watermelon Gazpacho with Guanciale, Feta and Arugula Sorbet, **68,** 69
Sous vide, 10
Speck
Red Beet Gnocchi with Hazelnut, Speck and Ricotta Salata, **84,** 85
Sweet Pea Soup with Roasted Ricotta, Speck and Honeysuckle, **78,** 79
Starters. See Appetizers and first impressions
Stocks
Beef Stock, 208
Chicken Stock, 209
Duck Wing Stock, 209
Fish Fumet, 209
homemade stock and good soup, 67
Lobster Stock, 210
preparation of, 10
Veal Stock, 213
Vegetable Stock, 213
Strawberries

Berry Juice, 208
Black Cod Fillet with Black Truffle, Serrano Ham, Figs and Amarone Zabaglione, 134, **135**
Halibut with Rhubarb-Strawberry Sauce, 118, 119
Radicchio and Strawberry Salad with Gorgonzola-Pistachio Truffles and Treviso, **46,** 47
Strawberry and Balsamic Mascarpone Gelato with Pink Peppercorns and Mint, **188,** 189
Watermelon, Berry, Pistachio Halva Salad, **198,** 199
Sunflower seeds
Honeyed Beet and Peach Salad with Whipped Goat Cheese, Sunflower Seed Praline and Raspberry Vinaigrette, **44,** 45

T

Teatro Goldoni, 1, 5
Tequila
Beef Carpaccio and Ubriaco Cheese, with Tropical Truffle and Tequila-Jalapeño Sauce, **28,** 29
Tomatoes and tomato juice
Best Chicken Ever 'Nilde," 154, **154–55**
Bigoli and Octopus with Amatriciana Sauce, **104,** 105
Brined Kurobuta Pork Chops with Black Cherry Sauce and Summer Vegetables, 148, **149**
Crazy Bubbling Tomato with Burratina and Green Pea Shoots, 50, 51
Deconstructed Tomatoes with Balsamic Jelly and Liquid Buffalo Mozzarella, 48, **49**
evolution of a tomato, 113
Fried Grouper with Tomato–Red Onion Marmalade and Pickled Celery, 170, 171
Lobster Risotto with Roasted Tomato and White Truffle Perfume, 98, 99
Octopus in Crustacean Sauce with Raisin Tomatoes, Smoked Potatoes and Summer Truffle Jam, **34,** 35
Prosciutto, Figs and Arugula with Tomato Marmalade and Parmesan Crisps, 20, 21
Sea Salt Bloody Mary, 13, 203, 204–5, **204**
Tomato–Red Onion Marmalade, 212
Tomato Sauce, 212
Tomato Water, 212
Tomato salt, sun-ripened, 13
Trapani salt, 13
Truffles, truffle juice, and truffle oil
Black Cod Fillet with Black Truffle, Serrano Ham, Figs and Amarone Zabaglione, 134, **135**
Endive and Frisée Popcorn Salad with Roasted Pear, Piave Cheese and Black Truffle, 42, **43**
Lobster Risotto with Roasted Tomato and White Truffle Perfume, 98, 99
Octopus in Crustacean Sauce with Raisin Tomatoes, Smoked Potatoes and Summer Truffle Jam, **34,** 35
Pan-Seared Black Grouper with Black Truffle Butter, Fava Beans and Smoked-Salt Fingerling Potatoes, 132, **133**
Truffle salt, black, 13
Turnips
Duck Breast with Sevruga Caviar, Kumamoto Oysters, Chive-Honey Sour Cream and Roots, **150,** 151
Ôra King Salmon with Beluga Lentils, Baby Turnips and Mustard Sauce, **120,** 121
Venison Tenderloin with Chestnut Grappa Sauce and Braised Root Vegetables, 152, **153**

V

Veal Stock, 213
Vegetable Stock, 213
Venetian world cuisine, 6
Venice, 1, 4, 117
Venison
Venison Glace, 215
Venison Tenderloin with Chestnut Grappa Sauce and Braised Root Vegetables, 152, **153**
Vinegar, 41

W

Washington, D.C., 1, 4, 5, 13
Watermelon
Watermelon, Berry, Pistachio Halva Salad, **198,** 199
Watermelon Gazpacho with Guanciale, Feta and Arugula Sorbet, **68,** 69
Wine
Black Cod Fillet with Black Truffle, Serrano Ham, Figs and Amarone Zabaglione, 134, **135**
cooking with a glass of wine and smile on your face, 4
Duck Fat–Poached Ahi Tuna with Orange Moscato Nectar, Foie Gras Stracciatella, Salsify Puree, **136,** 137
fish, wine to drink with, 117
John Dory with Garden Peas and Prosecco Nage, **130,** 131
Roasted Pear Soup with Chianti–Black Pepper Sorbet, 192, **193**
at Sea Salt and Barbatella, 207

Z

Zelaya, Liset, 203, 207, 216, **216**